Dialectical Behavior Therapy Skills Training with Adolescents

A Practical Workbook for Therapists, Teens & Parents

Jean Eich PsyD, LP

Copyright © 2015 by Jean Eich PsyD, LP

Published by
PESI Publishing and Media
PESI, Inc
3839 White Ave
Eau Claire, WI 54703

Cover Design: Amy Rubenzer
Layout: Bookmasters
Edited by: Blair Davis

Printed in the United States of America

ISBN: 978-1-937661-37-3

PESI
Publishing
& Media
www.pesipublishing.com

This book is dedicated to my mother, Judy, who during her life,
taught me many things, the utmost of which was to be silly and to trust myself.

Table of Contents

Acknowledgements

Thank you to Linda Jackson, Claire Zelasko, Blair Davis, and the rest of the PESI team. Your knowledge, skill, and enthusiasm have brought this book to life.

Special acknowledgement goes to Lane Pederson and Mark Carlson, owners of Mental Health Systems, PC. I am lucky and honored to have received training, support, and opportunities from you through the years. Thank you Steve Girardeau- your supervision, guidance, and friendship have shaped me into a better clinician and person. Thank you Janice Haines-Ross and Craig Roelke for your feedback on this book and for your support, camaraderie, and validation.

Thank you also to my family and friends, including my husband and best friend, Rob, my father, Jerry, my siblings Stephanie and Tony, and my aunt, Shirley. Your support has helped me complete this book and strive for great things.

Lastly, thank you to my clients- walking beside you on your journey has allowed me to see beauty and meaning in ways before unknown. May the things you've taught me continue to grow and be used to help others.

How to Use This Book

This book is a complete skills training manual for Dialectical Behavior Therapy (DBT) with adolescents and is focused on practical application for teens, parents and therapists. As a complete manual, this book has three audiences and consists of three parts.

Three Audiences

First, this book is for adolescents who are learning DBT in therapy or want to independently learn new skills to be more effective in a crisis, to regulate emotions, to improve relationships or to work on problem behaviors like isolation or fighting with others.

Second, this book is for the parents of adolescents who are learning DBT. Parents will learn tools to support their teen in using DBT at home, improve the relationship with their teen, and promote a consistent and effective household.

Third, this book is for therapists and can be used by them in several ways. This book can help therapists supplement what they are already doing in group or individual therapy with adolescents. It can also assist therapists in creating a new DBT program or to improve an existing one.

Three Parts

Part One includes teaching pages and worksheets for all four DBT skill modules. These pages teach each skill and ways to apply DBT skills. Part One is written for adolescents and includes examples to which teens can relate. Understanding the skills presented in Part One is also important for parents, and it is highly recommended that they read this section. Part One can also be useful for therapists, and these pages can be used in a skills group or individual therapy setting.

Part Two is written for parents. These chapters teach parents the basics of DBT, mindful parenting, self-care and effective communication. This section is intended to assist parents in finding balance in three key areas: allowing developmentally appropriate behaviors while addressing more serious behaviors, balancing rules with flexibility and balancing autonomy with structure and limits. Parents will also learn to avoid blaming themselves or others for mental health concerns. This will help parents focus on having influence (not control) over their teen to promote change. Part Two can also be helpful for therapists in working with parents of adolescents in therapy.

Part Three is written for therapists. Included in this section is information about running a DBT program, helping therapists bring to life DBT's functions and targets and create balance with adolescent-specific Dialectical Dilemmas. This section emphasizes the use of activities in teaching DBT skills to adolescents and describes activities for skills in all four DBT modules. It includes sample documents to assist in providing therapy. While therapists are the main audience for this section, both adolescents and parents can review and practice the activities listed.

This book is about helping the reader apply DBT skills and concepts. Readers interested in a more extensive discussion of adolescent DBT theory and interventions are referred to the book *Dialectical Behavior Therapy with Suicidal Adolescents* by Miller, Rathus & Linehan (2007).

About the Author

 **Jean Eich, PsyD, LP,** has provided DBT services for the better part of a decade at the largest DBT clinic in the Minneapolis/St. Paul area, where she has developed, facilitated and coordinated DBT programming for adolescents and their parents. Additionally, Dr. Eich has written curriculum and facilitated programming for adults with mental illness and developmental delays, and has helped to design and maintain studies examining clinical outcomes of DBT programs. She is also an adjunct assistant professor at St. Mary's University, and maintains a private practice in Maplewood, MN.

Foreword

Dialectical Behavior Therapy (DBT) has widely disseminated across clinical settings and populations for more than two decades, with interest in adolescent DBT being the most rapidly growing application of this evidence-based therapy. Until recently, DBT resources for teens have been few and far between, leaving therapists to adapt skills manuals clearly intended for adults or to figure it out on their own.

Among the adolescent manuals coming on the market, Dr. Jean Eich's *Dialectical Behavior Therapy Skills Training With Adolescents* stands out for its readability, instant applicability, and ease of use, among other distinctions. I have known Jean and her clinical work for the better part of a decade, so it comes as no surprise to me that she crafted a superb resource that will be a daily go-to for adolescent therapists everywhere. Since her doctoral internship at my DBT practice, Mental Health Systems (MHS), the largest DBT-specialized center in the Midwest, Jean has learned DBT for adults, adolescents, and other special populations in the trenches, both in adherent and adapted service deliveries. With broad experience, Dr. Eich has by turns been line therapist, consultant, trainer, program developer, university professor, and now author while branching out into her own private practice. Such a diversity of know-how from practitioner to instructor has made her well-suited to teach what she knows in such an accessible book.

Whereas other manuals focus more exclusively on adolescents as identified patients or the therapeutic process of DBT for therapists, this practical workbook wisely addresses three audiences in three distinct yet inter-related parts. **Part One** covers DBT for teens with comprehensive and age-relevant skills explanations, examples, and applied worksheets. Yet beyond the too-common bullet-point and text-driven psychoeducation on DBT skills, Dr. Eich makes the skills real for teens with exercises that get them *practicing* new behaviors. **Part Two** brings a dedicated focus to parents with pertinent information on DBT, parenting, and common teenage developmental issues, as well as, skills written to get parents using them individually, in connection with their child(ren), and as a part of the family system. This excellent section not only emphasizes that DBT skills can be used for anybody and everybody, but also that parents need to be active and involved in an effective change process. **Part Three** is crafted for therapists with practical advice on how to conduct DBT programming, how to navigate dialectical dilemmas with adolescent developmental tasks and behaviors, and how to balance therapy with parental involvement. In addition, Part Three contains superb suggestions for how to teach the skills in active and experiential ways along with helpful sample forms, handouts, and worksheets. While Part Three is not as comprehensive as other guides dedicated solely to therapists, it offers concise instructional and clinical gems either not found or buried deeply in other manuals.

Written to be used as an independent resource for teens and their parents or for use in combination with a DBT therapist or program, the book rates highly for its practicality, flexibility, and for making what can be a complex approach understandable to adolescents and parents that need these skills to realize better families and lives. As the author of three books on DBT, and as the trainer of over 7000 professionals on the approach, I can attest that therapists want resources that are meant to be pulled off the shelf, used, and perhaps never put back. Dr. Eich's manual meets and exceeds that standard; I am confident that a great many providers will find it to be an invaluable addition to their DBT libraries and practices.

Dr. Lane Pederson
Eden Prairie, Minnesota

About DBT®

Dialectical Behavior Therapy was created in the early 1990s by Dr. Marsha Linehan. Dr. Linehan originally created DBT as a treatment for adults who had difficulties with intense emotions and safety issues (like suicidal thoughts, attempts and self-injury) (Linehan, 1993a). She studied clients who went through DBT and found that it helped them to stay safe, act less impulsively and improve their emotions and relationships. Over the years, DBT has been proven helpful in a wide variety of settings and for a wide variety of people, including adolescents (Dimeff & Koerner, 2007; Marra, 2005; Miller, Rathus & Linehan, 2007).

Dialectical Behavior Therapy is a skills-based approach and includes four different modules, or sets, of skills (Linehan, 1993b). These modules include:

1. **Mindfulness:** Mindfulness skills improve awareness of one's self and the world. They teach you to make wise decisions, focus on one thing at a time, avoid judgments and do what works. These are considered *core* skills and are used with all other DBT skills.
2. **Distress Tolerance:** The Distress Tolerance module includes two subsets of skills: Crisis Survival and Accepting Reality skills. Crisis Survival skills are about coping with difficult situations without turning to harmful coping strategies like self-injury and drug use. Accepting Reality skills help you accept what cannot be changed so that you can focus on being effective.
3. **Emotion Regulation:** The Emotion Regulation module teaches skills to help you become more aware of your emotions, act in ways that reduce emotional suffering and create emotional balance through positive and confidence-building activities.
4. **Interpersonal Effectiveness:** The Interpersonal Effectiveness module teaches communication and relationship skills. These help you be assertive, build and keep healthy relationships and increase self-respect in relationships.

The DBT skills have unique names and acronyms. This helps you learn, remember and use the skills when you need them most. DBT skill names and acronyms also help us to have a common way of thinking and talking about skills. Many of the skills discussed in this book are based on Marsha Linehan's original work. Information from Miller, Rathus & Linehan's text on DBT with adolescents is also included. See the page titled "Source Citations for DBT Modules, Skills, Worksheets and Activities" at the end of this book for references to these works.

A DBT program typically involves a skills group and individual therapy. In a skills group, you learn what the skills are and get practice in using them. In individual therapy, you learn how to apply skills to your unique situation and to be aware of broader thought and behavioral patterns that contribute to mental health symptoms.

Teens and parents can use this book to learn and apply DBT independently. This book can also be used with a DBT program in a clinical setting. Teenagers who struggle with safety issues like suicidal ideation or self-harm need professional help, and in those situations, this book should only be used in addition to services by a licensed therapist.

Part One

DBT for Teens

Dialectics

The acronym *DBT* stands for Dialectical Behavior Therapy. You might be wondering, what does *dialectical* mean?

The main idea of dialectics is that there is an opposite of everything, and we tend to be the most effective when we can find balance between opposites. So, being dialectical means finding balance. We find this balance by incorporating, or including, ideas from two opposite ends of a spectrum (Linehan, 1993b).

For example, imagine spending 100% of your time on classes, homework and doing chores. Although you would get a lot done, spending all your time on these things would probably cause you to feel stressed, anxious and overwhelmed. After focusing so much on all this stress, you would likely get to a point where you wanted to run to the opposite end of the spectrum and spend 100% of your time having fun and goofing off. Going to this end of the extreme would be fun at first, but ignoring your responsibilities would eventually cause you do to poorly in school and might get you in trouble at home.

FUN	BALANCE	RESPONSIBILITIES

If we think about this problem dialectically, we would see that it is important to have fun *and* take care of our responsibilities. There are pros and cons to both having a good time and taking care of things we need to do, and when we can find a balance between the two, we are get the best of both worlds.

DBT teaches skills that help to us find balance not only between fun and responsibilities, but between a lot of other opposites, too. Remember, the idea is to find balance by incorporating *both* ends of the spectrum—not to end up at one extreme or the other.

Acceptance and Change

One very important dialectic in DBT is that of acceptance and change (Linehan, 1993b).

ACCEPTANCE	BALANCE	CHANGE

Acceptance

Acceptance means non-judgmentally understanding yourself, others and the world around you. When you accept something, you are not trying to change it but are instead just noticing it and taking it for what it is. Just because you accept something doesn't mean that you agree with it or like it. Instead, acceptance simply means that you understand what is.

For example, *self-acceptance* means accepting yourself just as you are. With self-acceptance, you are not doing anything differently but are focused on being non-judgmental and appreciating yourself as you are. The pro of this side of the dialectic is feeling positive and accepting about who you are. The downside is that there is no movement toward change, growth or improvement.

Change

On the opposite end of the dialectic is change. *Change* means doing something different or problem-solving to address something that is not working. When you are focused on change, you are not working on accepting or understanding but instead are focused on doing.

For example, *self-change* means changing something about you. With self-change, you are not focused on understanding but are instead focused on growing, learning and doing things differently. The pro of this end of the dialectic is that you are growing and improving. The downside is that you could feel uncomfortable or unaccepting toward yourself.

Balancing Acceptance and Change

Balancing acceptance and change means *both* accepting things as they are and creating change. In creating DBT, Dr. Linehan found that for therapy to be the most effective, you must work on change with an attitude of acceptance (Linehan, 1993b). In other words, to change, you must accept. DBT teaches skills that will help you with both acceptance and change. With the above example, this means accepting yourself as you are *and* focusing on ways you can change.

Mindfulness skills are really important in finding balance. This is because you can easily end up on an extreme end of a dialectic without realizing it. Mindfulness skills will help you notice where you are on a dialectic, and teaches ways to find balance.

Mindfulness Module

Mindfulness skills are *core* skills (Linehan, 1993b). This is because they are an important part of everything we do in DBT. We need mindfulness skills to make all the other DBT skills work the best. Being mindful means having *awareness*. This means being able to quiet our minds so that we can notice what is happening inside and what is happening outside of ourselves.

When we are *mindful*, we can:

• Notice our thoughts without being overwhelmed by them.

• Make planned decisions and avoid acting impulsively.

• Be focused on, appreciate and enjoy fun times.

• Feel more calm and relaxed, even in stressful situations.

• Use skills to help us act Effectively and feel better.

• _____

• _____

Mindfulness is the opposite of *mindLESSness*. When we are *mindless*, we:

• Don't notice our thoughts, which means they can get overwhelming and can increase anxiety, depression or anger.

• Are less likely to think about our decisions and can act impulsively.

• Are more likely to miss out on fun because we are worried or distracted.

• Will be more impacted by stressful situations.

• Might not be able to use skills when we really need them.

• _____

• _____

Mindfulness skills require lots of practice and may not come automatically at first. Remember that this is normal. Stick with it!

States of Mind

We will start the Mindfulness Module by discussing our three States of Mind. State of Mind is our outlook, or perspective. It has a big impact on what emotions we experience and the decisions that we make. DBT teaches three States of Mind: Emotion Mind, Wise Mind and Reason Mind (Linehan, 1993b).

EMOTION MIND   WISE MIND   REASON MIND

Emotion Mind

When we are in Emotion Mind, we are focused on our emotions. This means that our feelings are in charge, and our thoughts and behaviors are driven by them. We can be in Emotion Mind with both enjoyable and difficult emotions. In Emotion Mind, we are *not* focused on the facts and are instead just experiencing and focusing on feelings. Here are examples of situations that trigger Emotion Mind:

- Breaking up with your boyfriend or girlfriend

- Fighting with your parents

- Writing poetry

- Falling in love

- Listening to music

- _____

- _____

Reason Mind

When we are in Reason Mind, we are focused on the facts. This means that we are analyzing and thinking logically. In Reason Mind, our thoughts and behaviors are guided by facts. We are *not* focused on or feeling much emotion in Reason Mind. Here are some examples of situations that trigger Reason Mind:

- Solving a math problem

- Learning to drive

- Baking cookies

- Reading a book

- _____

- _____

Wise Mind

When we are in Wise Mind, we are able to feel our emotions *and* focus on the facts. In Wise Mind, we make decisions based both on how we feel and the facts. Wise Mind helps us do what is healthy and effective. Here are some examples of situations for Wise Mind:

- Doing homework before going out with friends

- Asking for help when frustrated with homework

- Using a DBT skill instead of acting on self-harm urges

- _____

- _____

Everyone has an Emotion Mind, a Reason Mind and a Wise Mind, and it is normal to be in each State of Mind at different times. For example, when falling in love, your thoughts and behaviors will likely not be focused on the facts but instead on your emotions. In math class, you will likely be focused on the facts so that you can solve a problem, and you will probably not be noticing your emotions.

Although it is normal to be in Emotion Mind and Reason Mind, it is important that we strive to be in Wise Mind. When we are in Wise Mind, we are best able to take care of ourselves and act effectively.

States of Mind Examples

This worksheet will help you learn more about Emotion Mind, Reason Mind and Wise Mind.

Read the following examples and think about which State of Mind each character might be in:

Isabelle woke up to the sound of her mom's voice saying, "ISABELLE!! GET OUT OF BED!" Isabelle turned over, looked at her clock and realized she was late. Knowing she didn't have much time, she stumbled out of bed and rushed through her morning routine. She didn't get to take a shower, didn't do her make up like she wanted and left the house in clothes she didn't feel good about. On the ride to school, Isabelle was feeling flustered and angry, and when her mom started asking her about the math test she took yesterday, she lost it. She didn't realize it at the time, but her body tensed up and her face got hot. Isabelle yelled at her mom, began crying and then refused to talk for the rest of the trip. When she got to school, she slammed the car door and decided to skip her first class.

What State of Mind was Isabelle in?

_____

How do you know she was in this State of Mind?

_____

Describe her thoughts:

_____

_____

Describe her body sensations:

_____

_____

Describe her actions:

_____

_____

Josh was waiting for biology, his favorite class, to start. The teacher came in and announced that they would be looking at a bug collection today. Josh heard moans and other students say, "Gross!" Josh doesn't like bugs, but he was too focused on what the teacher was saying to feel grossed out. During class, Josh looked at each bug and paid attention to its size and color. He took notes and highlighted things he thought might be on the test. When he was passed a sample of a cockroach, Josh briefly noticed an uneasy feeling in his stomach, but he ignored this and went back to his note-taking.

What State of Mind was Josh in?

_____

How do you know he was in this State of Mind?

_____

Describe his thoughts:

_____

_____

Describe his body sensations:

_____

_____

Describe his actions:

_____

_____

Kendra was sick, and her mom thought she needed to see a doctor. Kendra hated going to the doctor; it always made her so anxious. She noticed that just thinking about the doctor caused her heart to race, her palms to sweat and her stomach to feel upset. She had the urge to yell at her mom and refuse to see her doctor. Instead, Kendra told her mom, "I know I need to see the doctor, but I am really anxious." Kendra practiced deep breathing in the car on the way and distracted herself with Facebook® on her phone while in the waiting room. During the appointment, she held her mom's hand as the nurse swabbed her throat.

What State of Mind was Kendra in?

_____

How do you know she was in this State of Mind?

_____

Describe her thoughts:

_____

_____

Describe her body sensations:

_____

_____

Describe her actions:

_____

_____

States of Mind - Your Turn

Now it's your turn to think about when you have been in Emotion Mind, Reason Mind and Wise Mind.

Describe a time when you have been in Emotion Mind: _____

_____

_____

_____

_____

_____

What did you notice about your body when in Emotion Mind? _____

_____

_____

_____

What did you notice about your thoughts when in Emotion Mind? _____

_____

_____

_____

What did you notice about your behaviors or actions when in Emotion Mind? _____

_____

_____

_____

Describe a time when you have been in Reason Mind:_____

_____

_____

_____

_____

What did you notice about your body when in Reason Mind? _____

_____

What did you notice about your thoughts when in Reason Mind? _____

_____

_____

_____

What did you notice about your behaviors or actions when in Reason Mind? _____

_____

_____

_____

Describe a time when you have been in Wise Mind: _____

_____

_____

_____

_____

_____

What did you notice about your body when in Wise Mind? _____

_____

_____

_____

What did you notice about your thoughts when in Wise Mind? _____

_____

_____

_____

_____

What did you notice about your behaviors or actions when in Wise Mind? _____

_____

_____

_____

The "What" Skills

What do we do to get into Wise Mind? We use our Observe, Describe and Participate skills. We use these "What" skills to gather information so that we can understand the situation, make planned decisions and to help us use skills effectively (Linehan, 1993b).

Observe

When we Observe, we simply *notice*, or pay attention.

We can notice *external* events. External events are noticed through our five senses:

- Sight
- Taste
- Sound
- Touch
- Smell

We can also notice *internal* events. Internal events are things that happen inside your own mind or body. They include:

- Thoughts
- Body sensations
- Emotions
- Urges

When we Observe, we pay attention to external and internal events without holding on to them. This means we notice information and then let it go.

When we Observe, we decide where our attention goes.

This means we are making the decision to pay attention and not get caught up in one thought, emotion or experience.

Observing means watching our thoughts come and go, like clouds in the sky or waves in the ocean.

Describe

When we Describe, we give words to what we noticed.

Using words to Describe what we noticed help us communicate our experience to others and helps us to make sense what is happening.

It is important to avoid judgments when we Describe. Use words to describe the facts and make sure to call *a thought a thought, a feeling a feeling, an opinion an opinion* and so on.

A thought is a statement that runs through our head, such as, "I'm so dumb." This is just a thought and not a fact.

When using Describe, state, "I had the thought of 'I'm so dumb.'"

Describing a thought as a thought will keep you from mistaking a thought for a fact.

To Describe a feeling, use an emotion word, such as *happy*, *sad*, *scared* or *excited*. Sometimes when we feel an emotion, we skip the emotion word and jump right to what the emotion means to us. For example, we might say, "Math is the worst subject" when we feel frustrated.

When using Describe, state, "I feel frustrated with math."

Describing a feeling as a feeling will keep you from mistaking an emotion for a fact.

Opinions are views or thoughts that people have about something. Opinions are not facts, and people can see the same thing differently. Opinions are not right or wrong—they are just preferences. An example of an opinions is, "Video games are the best way to relax."

When using Describe, state, "It's my opinion that video games are a great way to relax."

Describing an opinion as an opinion will keep you from mistaking an opinion for a fact.

Participate

Participate means using the information we gathered with Observe and Describe to make effective decisions.

When we participate, we become a part of our experience. We are no longer just noticing—we are now acting.

Using our skills can be a way we participate.

It is common to Participate without using Observe and Describe, which means making decisions without first pausing to notice what is happening inside and outside of yourself.

Learning to first stop to Observe and Describe will help you Participate more effectively and make decisions from Wise Mind.

Observe, Describe & Participate: Put It Together

Here is an example of how Observe, Describe and Participate skills can be used together:

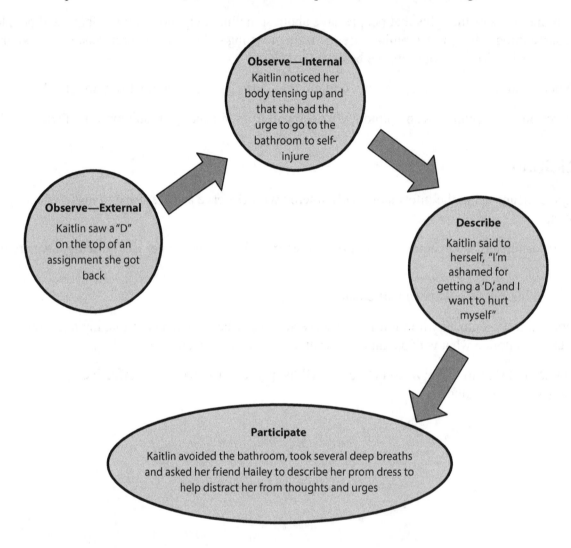

Observe—Internal
Kaitlin noticed her body tensing up and that she had the urge to go to the bathroom to self-injure

Observe—External
Kaitlin saw a "D" on the top of an assignment she got back

Describe
Kaitlin said to herself, "I'm ashamed for getting a 'D,' and I want to hurt myself"

Participate
Kaitlin avoided the bathroom, took several deep breaths and asked her friend Hailey to describe her prom dress to help distract her from thoughts and urges

Notice that Kaitlin avoided self injury because she was able to slow down to Observe and Describe her emotions, body sensations and thoughts. Observe and Described then helped her Participate with DBT skills.

The "What" Skills: Keep It Going

It is helpful to use your Observe, Describe and Participate skills even after you have Observed, Described and Participated. In other words, keep your "What" skills going!

Continuing to use the "What" skills will help you:

- Notice what worked and what did not work the first time.

- Continue to be aware of your emotions, body sensations, thoughts, urges or triggers.

- Apply more skills.

- _____

- _____

Take a look at the following example and how Kaitlin kept her "What" skills going:

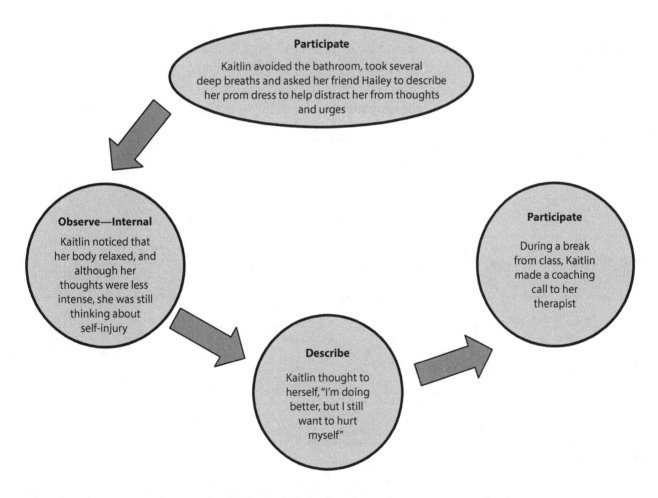

Participate
Kaitlin avoided the bathroom, took several deep breaths and asked her friend Hailey to describe her prom dress to help distract her from thoughts and urges

Observe—Internal
Kaitlin noticed that her body relaxed, and although her thoughts were less intense, she was still thinking about self-injury

Describe
Kaitlin thought to herself, "I'm doing better, but I still want to hurt myself"

Participate
During a break from class, Kaitlin made a coaching call to her therapist

Remember that you can keep your "What" skills going for as long as you need to!

One Minute to Observe & Describe

This worksheet will help you practice the Observe and Describe skills.

Observe and Describe skills require lots of practice. It works best to practice the Observe and Describe skills when we are calm and can really dedicate time and focus. Practicing when we are calm will make Observing and Describing more difficult situations easier.

During this exercise, think of your mind like a conveyor belt and do not let your mind get stuck on any one thing that you notice. Remember not to judge or evaluate what you notice. Instead, you are just taking the information in as it comes.

Follow these steps and then answer the questions below.

1. Get out a stopwatch or timer. (Tip: most cell phones have timers.)

2. Find a place to sit alone. Pick a location where you are not likely to be disturbed.

3. Set the stopwatch or timer for 1 minute.

4. Spend that minute using Observe and Describe. Try to pay attention to everything, notice things around you and notice what you are thinking or feeling. Remember to use your five senses.

When the timer goes off, answer the following questions to help you reflect on how Observe and Describe went.

What did you notice about your thoughts?

_____

_____

What did you notice about your body sensations?

_____

_____

What did you notice about your emotions?

_____

_____

What did you see?

_____

_____

What did you hear?

_____

_____

What did you feel?

_____

_____

What did you taste?

_____

_____

What did you smell?

_____

_____

Try this exercise several times. The more you practice Observe and Describe, the more aware you will become. Remember that practicing a new skill takes time, and you will get better the more you do it. For example, you can probably text much quicker now than you could the first time you tried it. That's how practice can help.

_____

_____

_____

_____

_____

_____

_____

_____

_____

_____

_____

_____

Observe, Describe & Participate Practice

Remember, practicing the "What" skills is important and will help you create a mindful mindset.

This worksheet will help you to put the Observe, Describe and Participate skills together.

Think of a difficult situation that you have recently experienced, such as a fight with a friend, having to give a speech in class or not getting invited to a party.

Observe and Describe—External: Write down what was happening in your environment, and include details.

Where were you?

_____

_____

Who was there?

_____

_____

What did you notice with your five senses (what did you see, hear, touch, smell and taste)?

_____

_____

Observe and Describe—Internal: Write down what was happening inside you, and include details.

What were you thinking?

_____

_____

How did your body feel?

_____

_____

What did you notice about your emotions?

_____

_____

What did you have the urge to do?

_____

_____

Participate: Write down what your actions or behaviors were, and include details.

How did you act, and what did you do?

_____

_____

Looking back, how could you have participated differently? (What could you have done differently?)

_____

_____

Try this exercise several times. You can use this worksheet to look back at a difficult situation in the past or while you are in a difficult situation. Remember, the goal is to be mindful in the moment. This will help you make planned and effective decisions when you participate.

_____

_____

_____

_____

_____

_____

_____

_____

_____

_____

_____

The "How" Skills

How do we use Observe, Describe and Participate to get into Wise Mind? We act non-judgmentally, one-mindfully and effectively.

Non-Judgmental Stance

Being Non-Judgmental means *focusing on the facts*. When we act Non-Judgmentally, we separate our opinions from the facts.

Remember: Facts are things that can be proven—or the who, what, when and where of a situation. Opinions, or judgments, are beliefs or thoughts about the facts.

Examples of judgments include:

• Right	• Wrong	• Good	• Bad	• Should	• Smart
• Stupid	• Pretty	• Ugly	• Fair	• Unfair	• Lazy

• _____   • _____   • _____

• _____   • _____   • _____

Using judgment words is often easier than describing the facts. The problem is, it's easy for us to see our judgments as facts.

When we are Non-Judgmental, we accept things as they are and avoid getting stuck on our opinions.

Having a Non-Judgmental Stance means identifying our emotions and opinions. In other words, a Non-Judgmental stance means that you do not mistake emotions and opinions for facts.

Judgments are a normal part of thinking and communicating and can be hard to avoid.
So, when you find yourself using judgments, don't judge yourself for it, just let the judgment roll by.

Non-Judgmental Stance Practice

It is common to use judgments and not even be aware of it. This exercise will help you identify your judgments and replace them with a Non-Judgmental Stance. Remember that a Non-Judgmental Stance means focusing on the facts and not mistaking your opinions or emotions for the facts.

Practice paying close attention to what you think and say, and record any judgments that you catch. Then brainstorm ways you can use a Non-Judgmental Stance instead.

Event	Judgment	Non-Judgmental Stance
Forgot my homework at home.	"I'm so stupid."	"I forgot my homework—it was a mistake. I feel embarrassed. Mistakes happen to everyone."

One-Mindfully

One-Mindfully means focusing on only one thing at a time.

Here are some examples of ways to be One-Mindful:

- When doing homework, only focus on homework.
- When watching TV, only watch TV.
- When talking to a friend, only talk to your friend.
- When you worry, only worry.

- _____
- _____

One-Mindfully can help us:

- Reduce anxiety and stress.
- Enjoy and get the most out of positive events.
- Accomplish and do a better job on tasks (like cleaning your room or doing homework).
- Show friends that you are interested in them.

- _____
- _____

To be One-Mindful, make a decision to focus your attention and block out distractions.

Here are four steps that can help you be One-Mindful:

1. Focus on one thing at a time.

2. Notice when you get distracted or your mind wanders.

3. Re-focus on one thing at a time.

4. Repeat steps 2 and 3 as often as needed.

Keep in mind that these steps are easy to understand but can be difficult to do. One thing that can help you with One-Mindfully is being aware of what tends distracts you. If you know what distracts you, you will be more likely to notice it when you are trying to be One-Mindful.

Some common distractions include:

- Worrying
- TV

- Cell phones
- People around you

- _____
- _____

- _____
- _____

It can take a lot of practice to be One-Mindful, so try not to get discouraged if it doesn't come easily.

One-Mindfully Practice

We live in a culture that is used to focusing on many things at once. This means being One-Mindful will take a lot of practice. Follow this exercise to help you practice One-Mindfully.

Remember that to be One-Mindful, you: 1) focus on one thing, 2) notice when you get distracted and 3) re-focus on one thing. You can repeat these steps as often as you need to.

In this exercise, you will be asked to pick an activity. Examples include watching a YouTube® video, texting a friend or going for a walk. Your activity can last a few minutes to an hour or more. We recommend starting with an activity that will take just a few minutes.

During this activity, your job is to be One-Mindful by only focusing on that one activity.

Don't judge yourself or quit if you get distracted. Instead, simply re-focus your mind back on your activity. You will probably have to re-focus many times. Remember that the more you practice One-Mindfully, the easier it will get!

After your activity, answer the following questions to help you process how it went.

My activity was: _____

_____

What did you notice about your activity? _____

_____

_____

_____

_____

During your activity, what did you get distracted by? _____

_____

_____

_____

What helped you stay One-Mindful? _____

_____

_____

_____

Effectively

Effectively means doing what works.

When we are Effective, we act as skillfully as possible.

To be Effective, make decisions that will help you meet your goals.

This means first figuring out what your goals are. When in a situation, consider what is important to you. Think about what you want now and in the long run.

Knowing what you want will help you decide how to act so that you can achieve your goal. For example, if your goal is to avoid self-injury, acting effectively would mean using distraction or asking for help to avoid acting on urges to self-injure.

Being Effective also means following the rules. This is because we can get into trouble when the rules are broken, which takes us further away from meeting our goals.

Sometimes emotions or judgments can keep us from being Effective. Acting Effectively means letting go of emotions and judgments that get in the way of doing what works.

Here are some examples of emotions and judgments that can get in the way:

- Anger.

- Resentment.

- Hurt.

- "This is not how it *should* be."

- "That's so <u>unfair.</u>"

- "That rule is just *stupid*."

- _____

- _____

When we let go of emotions and judgments that get in the way, we can really focus on our goals and do what works.

Effectively Examples

Remember that being Effective means doing what works. To be Effective, focus on what helps and avoid getting stuck on judgments or emotions. Remember to play by the rules, even when you disagree with them.

Read the following scenarios to figure out if the character in each story was effective or ineffective.

Situation 1: Jackie is standing in a very long lunch line. She's been in line for about 15 minutes and only has 15 minutes left in her lunch period. She finally gets to the front of the line and discovers the cooks ran out of what she wanted. Jackie will have to wait a couple more minutes for them to bring out new food. Jackie feels tired and angry and storms out of line saying, "I'll just have to go hungry today," even though she is the next person in line to be served.

What was Jackie's goal?

_____

Did how she act help her achieve her goal? Why or why not?

_____

_____

Was Jackie Effective?

_____

How did/could she focus on what works?

_____

Situation 2: Joe wants to go to his friend Brent's house on Saturday night. Brent recently switched schools, and Joe hasn't seen him in months, so Joe really wants to hang out and catch up. But, Joe's mom has to work late, and she wants Joe to babysit his little sister. Joe hates babysitting and thinks it's incredibly unfair that he has to give up his Saturday night for his sister. Usually, Joe will argue with his mom when she asks him to babysit, and he will end up giving her the silent treatment for days. This time Joe listens to his mom's side and suggests a compromise of having Brent come over instead of Joe going to Brent's house. Joe's mom agrees and even gives him money to order a pizza.

What was Joe's goal?

_____

Did how he act help him achieve his goal? Why or why not?

_____

_____

Was Joe Effective?

_____

How did/could he focus on what works?

_____

Situation 3: Your turn. Now describe a difficult situation that you have been in. Write down specifics about how your body felt, what your emotions were and how you decided to behave:

What was your goal?

_____

Did how you act help you achieve your goal? Why or why not?

_____

Were you Effective?

_____

How did/could you focus on what works?

_____

Mindfulness Module
Skills List

What skills:		
OBS	Observe	Pay attention—notice what is happening inside and outside yourself
DES	Describe	Give words to what you noticed
PART	Participate	Be active and engage in your experience
How skills:		
NJS	Non-Judgmental Stance	Focus on the facts—avoid labels or judgments
OM	One-Mindfully	Focus on one thing at a time—be in the here and now
EFF	Effectively	Do what works—use skills

Distress Tolerance Module

The Distress Tolerance module is full of skills that will help you deal with distress, or difficult and uncomfortable emotions. The idea is not to get rid of difficult emotions or to never have them again. Instead, the goal of this module is to *help you cope with difficult emotions* when they come up.

There are two subsets of skills in the Distress Tolerance module: Crisis Survival skills and Accepting Reality skills.

Crisis Survival Skills

The Distress Tolerance module starts with a set of skills that will help you survive, or get through, a crisis. A crisis is a very difficult or intense situation. Many people have trouble finding effective ways to deal with a crisis. Sometimes they turn to choices that help them get through the crisis but only make the situation worse or create problems in the long run.

Here are some examples of ineffective ways to deal with a crisis:

- Self-injury
- Drugs and alcohol
- Overeating
- _____
- _____
- _____

The cons of dealing with a crisis ineffectively can include:

- Hospitalization
- Conflict with others
- Poor health
- Guilt or shame
- _____
- _____
- _____

People turn to ineffective ways to cope because they do not yet have the skills they need to more effectively deal with a crisis. That is what the Crisis Survival skills are for.

The Crisis Survival skills are:

- Wise Mind ACCEPTS
- Self-Soothe
- IMPROVE the Moment
- Half-Smile
- Creative Outlet

Accepting Reality Skills

The other set of skills in the Distress Tolerance module are the Accepting Reality skills. These skills help you *focus on being Effective with accepting reality*, or with things that you cannot change.

Often, people will try to change things that they do not have control over. Putting your time and energy into trying to change things you can't change leaves you with little time and energy for things that you *can* change.

Accepting Reality skills will lower your distress and help you feel more in control. This is because you can focus on how to be effective and have energy for self-care.

The Accepting Reality skills are:

- Pros and Cons
- Turn the Mind
- Radical Acceptance
- Willingness

Crisis Survival Skills

A crisis is a difficult or intense event. Here are some examples of situations that might trigger a crisis:

- Failing a class
- Getting in a fight with friends
- Parents getting a divorce
- Being teased by classmates

- _____

- _____

- _____

An important part of Crisis Survival Skills is knowing when to take a break from the situation. Here are some questions that will help you decide if you need a break:

- Am I in Wise Mind?
- Are those involved in Wise Mind?
- Do I have what I need to fix or address the problem?
- Is this a good time to fix or address the problem?

If you answered "no" to any of these questions, it might be a good time to take a break and focus on something else.

When you stay in a crisis situation while in Emotion Mind, you will be more likely to act ineffectively, which will likely make the crisis worse or create more problems.

Crisis Survival requires *balance* between dealing with the crisis and taking a break.

Breaks are meant to be *planned* and *temporary*. This means it is important to mindfully take a break, and it is essential that you come back and deal with the crisis at some point.

Trying to *avoid* a crisis forever can cause the emotions to build up or allow for the crisis to get worse.

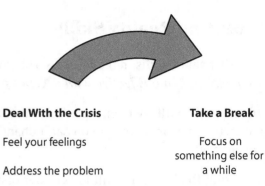

Deal With the Crisis

Feel your feelings

Address the problem

Take a Break

Focus on something else for a while

Wise Mind ACCEPTS

The Wise Mind ACCEPTS skill is often called "distract." This is because each letter in *ACCEPTS* stands for a way that you can distract yourself from a problem or crisis. Remember to make your distractions *planned* and *temporary*.

A—Activities

Distracting with Activities means keeping your mind and body busy. Here are some examples:

- Exercising
- Drawing or doodling
- Downloading songs
- Cleaning

- Computer games
- Doing nails/hair
- Rearranging your room

- Texting a friend
- Writing
- Playing with a pet

- _____
- _____

- _____
- _____

- _____
- _____

C—Contributing

Contributing means distracting yourself from your own problems by focusing on how to help someone else. This skill is most effective when you help others but do not take on their problems. Remember that you need to focus on yourself when you are in Wise Mind. Here are some examples of ways to Contribute:

- Make someone a card
- Call a grandparent
- Send someone a positive text

- Volunteer
- Do a chore for your parents

- Bake cookies for a friend
- Help a sibling with homework

- _____
- _____

- _____
- _____

- _____
- _____

C—Comparisons

Comparisons means distracting yourself from your own problems by comparing yourself to others who are in a worse situation. The goal is to put your situation in perspective and focus on what is going well for you. Be mindful and do not fall into self-judgment. If you notice yourself feeling bad, try another ACCEPTS skill. You can also use Comparisons to compare where you are now to where you have been in the past or use Comparisons to help you feel less alone by noticing that others are in a similar situation. Here are some examples of ways to use Comparisons:

- Compare yourself to characters on reality TV
- Compare your skill use now to when you first started DBT
- Notice how many people did worse than you on an assignment
- Listen to how others used skills

- _____ • _____
- _____ • _____

E—Emotions

Using Emotions to distract yourself means doing something to create a new feeling that will distract from the old emotion. The idea is to do things that may produce the opposite emotion of how you are feeling. Here are some examples of ways to use Emotions as a distraction:

- Watch a funny movie
- Do deep breathing
- Play sports
- Listen to happy music
- Look at funny websites
- Read inspirational quotes
- Watch inspiring videos on YouTube

- _____ • _____ • _____
- _____ • _____ • _____

P—Push Away

Push Away means distracting yourself by physically or mentally leaving a crisis or problem situation. Often Push Away can be used with one of the other ACCEPTS skills. Here are some examples:

- Imagine your worries are bubbles you can pop
- Write down your thoughts and tear them up
- Sit outside
- Block out thoughts about the crisis
- Take a walk

- _____ • _____
- _____ • _____

T—Thoughts

We can distract ourselves by changing our thoughts or adding thoughts that have nothing to do with stressors. For example, try not to think about a pink elephant. What happened? You probably thought about a pink elephant. The way to not think about a pink elephant is to instead think about a purple giraffe. Telling yourself not to think about your problems just causes you to think about them. To avoid thinking about problems or a crisis, think about something else. Here are some examples:

- Count to 100
- Sing your favorite song
- Name an animal for every letter of the alphabet

- Imagine what you would do if you won the lottery
- Count how many blue things you see

- _____
- _____

- _____
- _____

S—Sensations

We can use our five senses to distract. The idea is to distract yourself from stressors by awakening one of your senses. This is different from the Self-Soothe skill (which you will learn next), because the goal is not for your senses to be soothed, but instead for the sensation to be strong enough that you have to focus on it. Here are some examples of how to use Sensations as a distraction:

- Hold an ice cube
- Take a hot shower

- Eat spicy food
- Squeeze a stress ball

- Suck on a sour candy
- Look at bright colors

- Listen to loud music
- Sniff strong perfume

- _____
- _____

- _____
- _____

- _____
- _____

- _____
- _____

Self-Soothe

The Self-Soothe skill means using your five senses to *comfort and nurture* yourself (Linehan, 1993b). Instead of waiting for someone else to nurture or comfort you, with Self-Soothe, you can comfort yourself. This is helpful because other people will not always be available when you need them. Learning to Self-Soothe will help you take care of yourself, no matter who is around. There are many ways to Self-Soothe. Here are some ideas for each sense:

Vision

- Look at old pictures
- Do your nails or hair

- Read old letters
- Look at art

- Look at beautiful pictures on Tumblr®
- Gaze at the stars

- Notice flowers
- Draw

- _____
- _____

- _____
- _____

- _____
- _____

- _____
- _____

Hearing

- Listen to instrumental music
- Listen to the birds
- Call a friend
- Listen to the rain
- Tune in to your favorite radio station
- Sing a song
- Turn on a sound machine

- _____
- _____
- _____
- _____
- _____
- _____
- _____
- _____

Smell

- Use a scented lotion
- Bake cookies
- Use perfume or body spray
- Light a candle
- Get aromatherapy oils
- Smell flowers
- Notice fresh-cut grass

- _____
- _____
- _____
- _____
- _____
- _____
- _____
- _____

Taste

- Have a piece of chocolate
- Chew gum
- Drink tea
- Get a bag of chips
- Eat strawberries or other fruit
- Have a scoop of ice cream
- Suck on a mint

- _____
- _____
- _____
- _____
- _____
- _____

Touch

- Use a favorite lotion
- Take a bubble bath
- Wear a soft sweatshirt
- Hold a stuffed animal
- Play with Silly Putty® or Play Dough®
- Put soft sheets on your bed
- Get a massage

- _____
- _____
- _____
- _____
- _____
- _____

IMPROVE the Moment

The goal of the IMPROVE the Moment skill is to replace negative events with more positive ones (Linehan, 1993b). Each letter in *IMPROVE* stands for a way to improve your thoughts or physical sensations so that the moment you are in becomes easier to handle.

I—Imagery

Imagery means using your imagination to create a different situation that feels more comfortable and safe. Imagery works best when you include your five senses. Here are some ways to use Imagery:

- Imagine being on the beach
- Imagine a safe place
- Imagine your ideal self
- Imagine being skillful/meeting your goals
- Listen to guided imagery
- Remember a favorite time

- _____
- _____
- _____
- _____
- _____
- _____

M—Meaning

Using the Meaning skill means finding a purpose or reason for what you are going through. Finding or making meaning can help a crisis become more manageable. Here are some ways to use Meaning:

- "Going through this will make me a strong person."
- "There is a silver lining in this crisis."
- "Having this experience will help me understand others."
- "This will help me learn new skills."
- "If I hadn't changed schools, I wouldn't have met my best friend."

- _____
- _____

- _____
- _____

P—Prayer

Using the Prayer skill means connecting to something greater and opening yourself to the moment. You do not have to be spiritual or religious to use Prayer, and Prayer can mean something different to everyone. Here are some ways to use Prayer:

- Say a religious prayer
- Go to a church service
- Read the Bible or another religious book
- Meditate
- Take a walk and connect with nature
- Listen to inspiring music

- _____
- _____
- _____

- _____
- _____
- _____

R—Relaxation

To goal with the Relaxation skill is to help your body feel more comfortable and calm. When your body is calm, your mind will be likely to be calm, too. Here are some ways to use Relaxation:

- Take a hot bath or shower
- Do deep breathing
- Meditate
- Take a walk
- Drink hot tea
- Do some stretches
- Try yoga
- Do a word search puzzle
- Cuddle with a pet

- _____
- _____
- _____

- _____
- _____
- _____

O—One Thing at a Time

To use the One Thing at a Time skill, remind yourself to focus on one thing and that you do not have to take on everything at once. Here are some ways to use One Thing at a Time:

- Say, "I only need to survive this moment."
- Remind yourself, "One day at a time."
- Do a puzzle and only focus on the puzzle
- Make a list and work on only the first task

- _____
- _____

- _____
- _____

V—Vacation

The Vacation skill means taking a break from your stressors for a while. Just like when you take a real vacation, the Vacation skill is about having fun and getting out of the day-to-day routine. With the Vacation skill, your Vacation should last no more than one day. Here are some ways to use Vacation:

- Spend a day at the mall
- Get a manicure/pedicure
- Do a new art project
- Go to a new restaurant and order a dessert you have never had
- Go mini-golfing
- Go to a movie

- _____
- _____
- _____
- _____

E—Encouragement

When you use the Encouragement skill, you become your own cheerleader. This means you root yourself on, especially during stressful times. Here are some ways to use Encouragement:

- Make a list of your positive qualities
- Listen to a song that will pump you up
- Tell yourself, "I can do it!" or "I am strong!"
- Give yourself credit for successes, no matter how small

- _____
- _____
- _____
- _____

Half-Smile

The Half-Smile skill is similar to the Improve the Moment skill. With Half-Smile, you can change your emotions and reduce stress by putting just a slight smile on your face (Linehan, 1993b).

There is a strong connection between your body and emotions. Your body associates smiling with feeling happy. So, mindfully doing a Half-Smile will remind you of feeling happy, and can help to lift your mood.

To do a Half-Smile, sit still and relax your face muscles, and try not to put an expression on your face. Notice how it feels to have your face relaxed and expressionless. Next, slightly smile and notice how your face feels. Focus on making your face look calm and peaceful (Linehan, 1993b). If it helps, think about something that helps you feel peaceful and joyful.

You can use a Half-Smile any time you want or need to.

Use a Half-Smile when you are feeling alright and when you are having a difficult time. Here are some suggestions for times to use Half-Smile:

- Half-Smile when you are getting ready for school in the morning.
- Half-Smile when listening to music.
- Half-Smile before you fall asleep at night.
- Half-Smile when you feel annoyed.
- Half-Smile when you feel disappointed.
- Half-Smile before sending a text or email.

Creative Outlet

The Creative Outlet skill is about using your emotional energy to be creative.

Everyone has a creative side, and you do not have to be a skilled artist to use the Creative Outlet skill. Creativity differs for each person, and it's important to find an activity that works for you. Here are some examples of Creative Outlets:

- Drawing or doodling
- Writing poetry or short stories
- Coloring
- Playing an instrument
- Writing a song
- Playing with clay or Play Dough®
- Singing
- Dancing
- Collage-making
- Doing your hair, nails or makeup
- Designing clothes or putting together outfits
- Designing video games
- Woodworking
- _____
- _____
- _____
- _____
- _____

Remember that the Creative Outlet skill is a Crisis Survival skill, and it is important to use it to focus away from the crisis. Use the Creative Outlet skill to put your emotional energy into creativity rather than getting stuck in a crisis or difficult emotions.

Do I Need A Break?

Remember that Crisis Survival is about taking a break when you need one. Taking a break when you are in Emotion Mind will help you regroup and decompress, so when you do approach the problem or crisis, you will be more effective. This worksheet will help you figure out if you should take a break.

Am I in Wise Mind?

Here are some questions that will help you determine which State of Mind you are in.

How does your body feel?

_____

If you have intense body sensations, such as tight muscles, racing heart or rapid breathing, it is likely a good time to take a break.

What are your thoughts like?

_____

If your thoughts are negative, aggressive, blaming or over-focused on your worries, it is likely a good time to take a break.

What do you have the urge to do?

_____

If you have the urge to self-injure, act on suicidal thoughts, use drugs or alcohol, yell, act aggressively or shut down, it is likely a good time to take a break.

How are you communicating?

_____

If you are communicating angrily or are giving someone the silent treatment, is likely a good time to take a break.

Are the others I'm interacting with in Wise Mind?

What do you notice about others' body language?

_____

If those involved appear tense, are clutching their fists, are crying or otherwise look highly emotional, it may be a good time to take a break.

How are those involved communicating?

_____

If those involved are yelling or are shut down, it may be a good time to take a break.

Do I have what I need to fix or address the problem?

What skills can you use to address the problem?

_____

Do you have what you need to use these skills?

_____

If you cannot think of skills to use or do not have what you need to use those skills, it may be a good time to take a break.

Is this a good time to fix or address the problem?

Do you have enough time to address the problem?

_____

Is there another time that would be better?

_____

If there is another time that would be better or you do not have enough time to deal with the problem, it might be good to take a break.

Complete the next worksheet, My Crisis Survival Plan, to be prepared to take a break with Distress Tolerance skills.

My Crisis Survival Plan

It is time for me to turn to my Crisis Survival skills when:

1. _____
2. _____
3. _____
4. _____
5. _____

This is how I can use the **Wise Mind ACCEPTS** skill to deal with my crisis:

1. _____
2. _____
3. _____

This is how I can use the **Self Soothe** skill to deal with my crisis:

1. _____
2. _____
3. _____

This is how I can use the **IMPROVE the Moment** skill to deal with my crisis:

1. _____
2. _____
3. _____

This is how I can use the **Creative Outlet** skill to deal with my crisis:

1. _____
2. _____

I can also use a **Half-Smile** to deal with my crisis.

These are people I can call for support:

1. Name: _____   Phone Number: _____
2. Name: _____   Phone Number: _____
3. Name: _____   Phone Number: _____

I commit to follow my Crisis Survival Plan. If I cannot keep myself safe, I commit to call 911.

_____   _____
Signature   Date

Accepting Reality Skills

An important idea in DBT is pain versus suffering.

Pain	Suffering
• Pain is normal, and everyone experiences emotional or physical pain at times • Pain is a part of life and cannot be avoided • Pain is temporary and will come and go	• Suffering is common but does not have to happen • Suffering can be avoided • Suffering lasts longer than pain

Suffering is what happens when you do not deal with or accept pain (Linehan, 1993b).

Here are some examples of how pain can turn into suffering:

- Pretending like everything is Ok when it is not
- Ignoring or bottling up your emotions
- Thinking or talking about a crisis or difficult event over and over
- Not asking for help when you know you need it
- Ignoring problems
- Focusing a lot on trying to change other people
- Blaming yourself or other people for difficult situations
- Not talking about your emotions
- Not letting yourself see the positives
- Only thinking about or focusing on pain

- _____

- _____

The second half of the Distress Tolerance module is about helping you accept reality. When you can accept reality, or what is, you can avoid suffering.

We will talk more about pain and suffering when we get to the Emotion Regulation module.

Pros & Cons

Pros and Cons is a skill that helps us better understand reality. This is because we are looking at the Pros (or benefits) and the Cons (or costs) of our actions.

Sometimes it can be hard to look at the Pros and Cons of a behavior, because we get used to looking at some actions as "bad." A good example of this is self-injury, which often comes with negative judgments. Remember that there are benefits, or reasons, for every behavior. The goal of Pros and Cons is to look objectively (or without judgment) at the benefits and costs of decisions. This means seeing *both* the Pros and Cons.

The Pros and Cons skill can:

1. Help you make more mindful and planned decisions.
2. Help you look past actions so you can decide if you want to do the same thing next time.

There are many ways to use the Pros and Cons skill. One option is to look at the short- and long-term Pros and Cons of a behavior or action.

Take a look at the following example, which lists the Pros and Cons of skipping school.

	Pros	Cons
Short Term	• Get to sleep in • Don't have to feel anxious about going to class • Get to avoid peers who annoy me	• Will miss the lesson • Don't get the homework • Really won't want to go to class tomorrow
Long Term	• Know my anxiety will go down if I skip school	• Will be really confused about class • Will miss a bunch of assignments • Could fail the class • Possible detention

Another option is to look at the Pros and Cons of doing an action or not doing an action.

Take a look at the next example, which looks at the Pros and Cons of going to a party.

	Pros	Cons
Go to Party	• Can hang out with my friends • Could make new friends • Might be fun	• Will be anxious • There could be alcohol there • People I don't know will be there
Don't Go to Party	• Can spend time at home • Don't have to feel anxious • No pressure to drink	• Not as much fun at home • Won't see my friends • No chance to make new friends

Pros & Cons - Your Turn

Now it's your turn to practice Pros and Cons. Try both types of Pros and Cons lists!

This is a Pros and Cons list about: _____

	Pros	Cons
Short Term		
Long Term		

This is a Pros and Cons list about: _____

	Pros	Cons
Do Behavior		
Don't Do Behavior		

Radical Acceptance

Radical Acceptance means accepting reality, no matter what reality is.

Trying to change things that you have no control over leads to suffering. You waste your time and energy when you try to change things that cannot be changed.

Radical Acceptance means accepting what you cannot change, so you can spend your time and energy on things that you can *change.*

When you stop fighting what you cannot change, you can accept reality.

Consider what you can and cannot change:

What I CANNOT Change	What I CAN Change
• The past	• My skill use
• Other people	• How long I focus on things
• Rules and laws	• Who I spend my time with
• Death, divorce or loss	• My own decisions
• Who my family is	• My attitude
• _____	• _____
• _____	• _____
• _____	• _____
• _____	• _____

Acceptance means *understanding reality*.

Acceptance is NOT:

- Giving up

- Agreeing with the way things are

- Approving of or liking the situation

- Weakness

- Failure

Radical Acceptance does not mean that you have failed or that you have to put up with a hurtful situation. Radical Acceptance instead is about using your time and energy in a way that helps you move forward.

Turn the Mind

The Turn the Mind skill is about changing your thoughts so that you can Radically Accept.

Working on acceptance is like being at a fork in the road (Linehan, 1993b).
One fork leads to Radical Acceptance. The other fork leads to suffering.

You can make a *choice* about which path to take
Your choice is made by *how you think* about reality.

To avoid suffering, you need to practice Turning your Mind toward acceptance *over and over*.

Here is an example of what taking the fork toward suffering looks like:

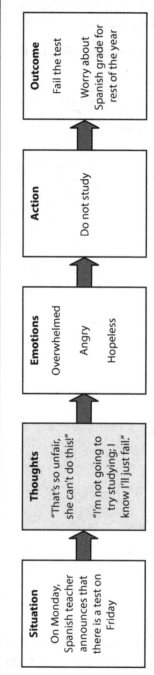

Situation	Thoughts	Emotions	Action	Outcome
On Monday, Spanish teacher announces that there is a test on Friday	"That's so unfair, she can't do this!" "I'm not going to try studying; I know I'll just fail."	Overwhelmed Angry Hopeless	Do not study	Fail the test Worry about Spanish grade for rest of the year

Remember, we can't always change our situation, but we can make the choice to turn our thoughts toward Radical Acceptance:

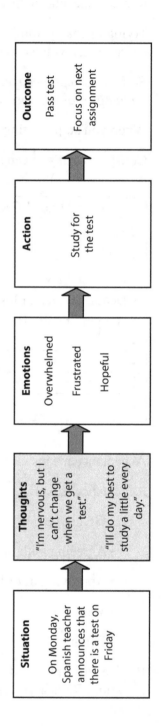

Situation	Thoughts	Emotions	Action	Outcome
On Monday, Spanish teacher announces that there is a test on Friday	"I'm nervous, but I can't change when we get a test." "I'll do my best to study a little every day."	Overwhelmed Frustrated Hopeful	Study for the test	Pass test Focus on next assignment

Turn the Mind - Your Turn

Our thoughts have a big impact on our ability to Radically Accept. It can be easy to get into thought patterns that lead us down the path of suffering. With this exercise, you will get to practice paying attention to your thoughts and turning them toward acceptance.

Pick a situation where you have difficulty using Radical Acceptance. Fill in how you are thinking and how your thoughts impact your emotions and behaviors:

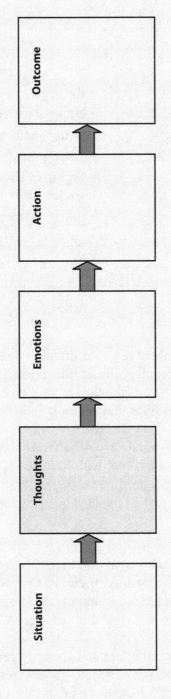

Now practice Turn the Mind to think about the same situation in a way that helps you to use Radical Acceptance:

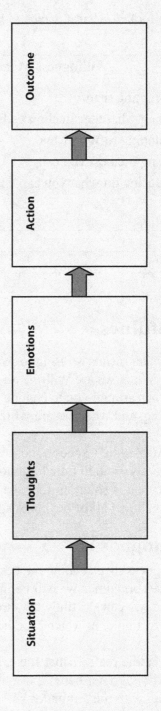

Willingness & Willfulness

Willingness and Willfulness are attitudes that we can take toward difficult situations.

Take a look at what it means to be Willing or Willful:

Willingness Means . . .	Willfulness Means . . .
• Accepting reality • Doing what the situation calls for • Listening to Wise Mind • Doing the best you can • Focusing on what you can change • _____ • _____ • _____	• Refusing to accept reality • Doing what you want, regardless of if it works • Being stubborn • Giving up • Trying to change things you know you can't change • _____ • _____ • _____

Willfulness

Willfulness means refusing to participate effectively in a situation that is difficult, you dislike or feel is unfair. When we are Willful, we are not accepting life as it is. Sometimes, Willfulness means expecting the things around you to change rather than you adapting to your environment. Willfulness leads to suffering, and when we are willful, we feel stuck. Take a look at this example:

At Maddie's school, there is only a 5-minute break between classes. She hates this because it is barely enough time to go to the bathroom, chat with her friends and walk to her next class. Maddie feels it is so unfair that she protests by ignoring the bell between classes. This causes her to be late to almost all of her classes, and after just a few days of being late, she ends up in detention.

Willingness

Willingness means doing the best you can with what you have. This requires Radical Acceptance, because sometimes we will be in situations that are difficult or that we feel are unfair. When we are Willing, we can skillfully get through difficulties and might even learn and grow from them. Take a look at this example, in which Maddie uses Turn the Mind and practices Willingness:

Maddie realizes that she cannot change the fact that she only gets 5 minutes between classes. Although her belief that it is unfair has not changed, she accepts that she needs to do the best she can with the 5 minutes she is given. She focuses on taking the quickest route between classes and starts meeting with her friends after school to catch up.

Distress Tolerance Module Skills List

The Distress Tolerance module teaches skills that will help you deal with distress, or difficult and uncomfortable emotions. Remember that the goal is not to get rid of difficult emotions or to never have difficult emotions again. Instead, the goal of the Distress Tolerance module is to *help you cope with difficult emotions* when they come up.

Crisis Survival skills:		
DIST	Wise Mind ACCEPTS	Distract yourself, focus away from what is stressful
SS	Self-Soothe	Use your five senses to feel comforted and nurtured
ITM	IMPROVE the Moment	Replace difficult events with enjoyable events
HS	Half-Smile	Put a small smile on your face
CO	Creative Outlet	Put your emotional energy into creativity
Accepting Reality skills:		
P&C	Pros and Cons	List the pros and cons
RA	Radical Acceptance	Accept what cannot change; focus on what can
TTM	Turn the Mind	Change your thoughts so that you can accept
WI	Willingness	Do the best you can with what you have

Emotion Regulation Module

The Emotion Regulation module is about learning to *understand and balance your emotions.*

The Emotion Regulation module teaches skills that can help you (Linehan, 1993b):

- Observe and Describe your emotions

- Reduce your vulnerability with Emotion Mind

- Increase positive emotions

- Avoid emotional suffering

- Act effectively when feeling difficult emotions

- _____

- _____

Emotions can be complicated and confusing.

Emotions can also be enjoyable and are a big part of what makes us human.

It's normal to have conflicted feelings and opinions about having emotions. It can be helpful to think and talk about how you see your emotions.

Let's start by looking at the Pros and Cons of emotions:

Pros	Cons
• Can feel emotions like happiness, love, excitement.	• Have to feel uncomfortable emotions like anger, sadness, hurt.
• Emotions help me empathize with others.	• Emotions can be overwhelming and confusing.
• Emotions help me get in touch with my creative side.	• Emotions can come with urges.
• _____	• _____
• _____	• _____
• _____	• _____
• _____	• _____
• _____	• _____

What Do You Believe About Emotions?

It is common for people to have beliefs about emotions that are not true. The way we think about emotions changes the way we experience and express them. Sometimes, how we see emotions can be ineffective and could create suffering. This is why it is important to examine your beliefs about emotions. Take a look at this list of misconceptions about emotions. Check the ones that fit for you.

- ☐ Sometimes I have the wrong emotion.

- ☐ I must be weak if I feel sad or anxious.

- ☐ Some emotions are bad.

- ☐ If I feel my feelings, I'll act out of control.

- ☐ If I feel bad, it must mean something is wrong with me.

- ☐ If I'm the only one who has this emotion, I shouldn't be feeling how I feel.

- ☐ It is Ok to ignore painful or difficult emotions.

- ☐ Being emotional is the only way to get support from others.

- ☐ Other people know how I'm feeling better than I do.

- ☐ I am a bad person because I feel depressed (or worthless, guilty, anxious, etc.).

- ☐ I must be doing something wrong if I feel bad.

- ☐ I'm supposed to always feel happy.

- ☐ People won't like me if they really know how I'm feeling.

- ☐ I have to yell when I'm angry.

- ☐ I shouldn't feel emotions.

- ☐ _____

- ☐ _____

- ☐ _____

Take a look at the next page, "Emotions: The Basics," to learn more about why statements like the ones on this list are untrue.

Emotions: The Basics

Emotions are not positive or negative, good or bad, right or wrong. Sometimes we call emotions like sadness or anger "bad" because we dislike them. However, all emotions are a normal part of being human, and there is no right or wrong way to have them. Judging emotions as good or bad can create suffering, because it can keep us from feeling our feelings. It is more effective to think of emotions as comfortable or uncomfortable, enjoyable or difficult.

You are not your emotion. Sometimes when we experience the same emotion a lot, we can mistake that emotion for a part of our identity. For example, saying "I am depressed" is like saying that you are depression. Remember that emotions are only a part of who you are. Feeling a difficult emotion does not mean that you *are* the difficult emotion, so instead of saying "I am depressed," say "I feel depressed." Also, feeling difficult emotions does not mean that there is something wrong with you or that you have done something wrong.

You cannot get rid of emotions. Sometimes people try to stuff, ignore or bottle up difficult feelings. For example, we can think things like "I shouldn't feel sad any more" or "no one else is this upset." We can't force ourselves to not have emotions. Avoiding or stuffing emotions just causes them to stick around longer. Radically Accepting difficult emotions works better than trying to get rid of them.

Emotions do not last forever. When we experience the same emotion often, it can be easy to think "I'm always going to feel sad" or "I'm never going to get over this." Remember that emotions naturally come and go. Sometimes we keep the same emotion around by ruminating or behaving in ways that keep the emotion activated. Emotions will eventually pass, and we can use skills to tolerate them and to create new emotions, too.

Emotions are not facts. Emotions, especially when intense, can feel like the "truth." In other words, when we have a strong emotion, we might see thoughts and beliefs associated with that emotion as the only possible truth. However, emotions are not facts and do not prove our thoughts and beliefs. For example, when you feel disappointed, you might start to believe "the world is against me." Sometimes we can mistake emotions as evidence and our belief can feel true.

You can have an emotion and not act on it. It is normal to have urges associated with emotions. For example, when we feel angry, we might think "when I'm mad I have to yell." Although urges associated with an emotion can be strong, you can make a choice if you want to act on your urge. Even with intense emotions, you do not have to act on your urges.

Your emotions are unique to you. All people are capable of the same emotions, but people can have different emotions in response to the same situation. Each person can also experience the same emotion differently. For example, some people feel anxiety in their chest, and some, in their stomach.

Why Do We Have Emotions?

Emotions have played a big part in our survival as a species. When humans lived in the wild, being afraid would prevent us from going places that were dangerous and help us avoid animals that could cause us harm. Being angry would help humans fight when faced with a predator. Feeling love would help us find a partner and keep the human species going.

Emotions still have an important place in our lives, even though we have come a long way since living in the wild. Following are some reasons we have emotions.

Communication. Emotions help us share our experiences with others (Linehan, 1993b). Emotions can come across in verbal (e.g., yelling, speaking softly, giggling) and nonverbal communication (e.g., eye contact, slouching, smiling). When emotions are involved in the way we communicate, other people can more quickly and easily understand what we are trying to share.

Connections With Others. Emotions help us to empathize with, understand and appreciate other people. When others show you empathy, you are likely to feel connected to them. Emotions help us create more meaningful connections with others.

Motivation. Emotions help us be motivated and accomplish tasks (Linehan, 1993b). For example, being moderately angry might help you assert yourself. Emotions can also help us save time in how we respond to a situation. For example, when startled, you will quickly move out of the way of danger. You don't even think about moving—your emotions and body just take over.

Wise Mind. Emotions are a very important part of our Wise Mind. Emotions can be signals or alarms that tell us there is something we should pay attention to (Linehan, 1993b). This "gut feeling" is an important part of Wise Mind and can help us act effectively.

Primary & Secondary Emotions

We can experience more than one emotion in reaction to a single event.

First, we experience a Primary Emotion. A Primary Emotion is a reaction to a triggering event (Linehan, 1993b). A triggering event is something that happened in the environment that created, or triggered, an emotion.

Here are some examples of triggering events:

- Having a first kiss

- Getting a D on an assignment

- Hearing your mom say "no" to a request

- Scoring a goal at a soccer game

- _____

- _____

- _____

Primary Emotions are "hard wired," meaning they are like a reflex. Primary Emotions happen quickly and naturally. Primary Emotions can be like smoke detectors; they can alert us to something to which we need to pay attention.

Here is an example of how an event might trigger a Primary Emotion:

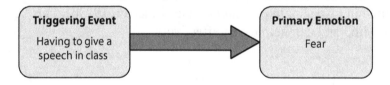

Having emotions might be less complicated if we only had Primary Emotions, but, we don't just have Primary Emotions, we also have Secondary Emotions.

Secondary Emotions are created by the way we think about our reactions to triggering events. In other words, Secondary Emotions are feelings about Primary Emotions. They are not "hard wired."

Here is an example of how an event might trigger Primary and Secondary Emotions:

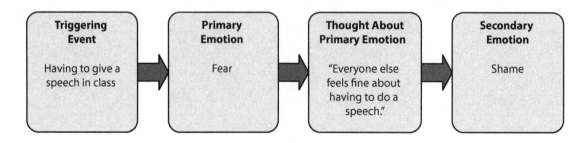

Primary & Secondary Emotions - Your Turn

This worksheet will help you look at your Primary and Secondary Emotions.

Remember:

• A Primary Emotion is the first emotion that you feel when an event happens.

• A Secondary Emotion is a reaction to a Primary Emotion.

Think of a triggering event in your past. Keep in mind that your triggering event could be either enjoyable or difficult. After remembering your triggering event, think about the very first emotion you had. This was your Primary Emotion. Next, consider how you were thinking about your Primary Emotion and write your thoughts in the "Reaction to Primary Emotion" box. Finally, remember how you were feeling after this thought and put it down as your Secondary Emotion.

If trying to look back at a past triggering event isn't working, notice a current situation and do this exercise in the moment.

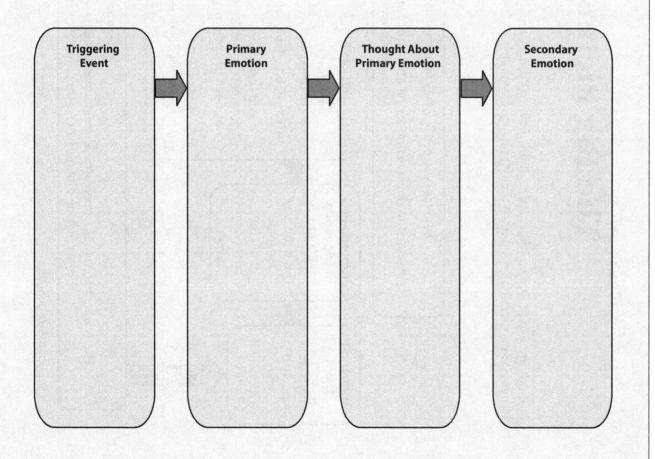

The Big Picture of Emotions

Emotions are even more complicated than just having Primary and Secondary Emotions. Our bodies, the way we communicate and our actions are all also a part of the big picture of emotions. Here is a model that can help explain how emotions are created.

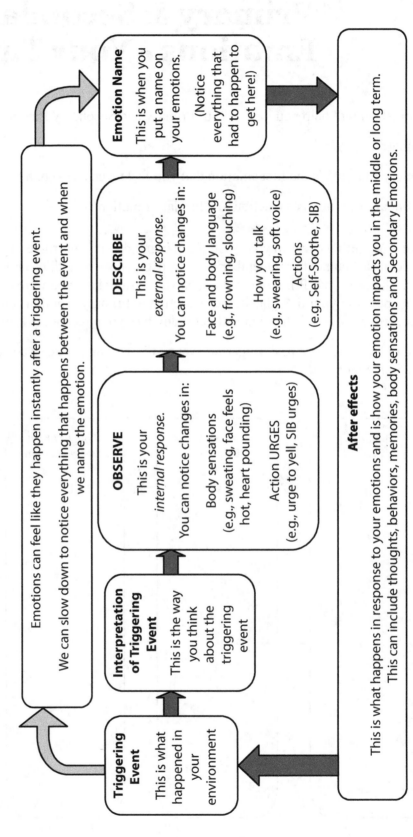

Emotions can feel like they happen instantly after a triggering event.

We can slow down to notice everything that happens between the event and when we name the emotion.

Triggering Event

This is what happened in your environment

Interpretation of Triggering Event

This is the way you think about the triggering event

OBSERVE

This is your *internal response.*

You can notice changes in:

Body sensations
(e.g., sweating, face feels hot, heart pounding)

Action URGES
(e.g., urge to yell, SIB urges)

DESCRIBE

This is your *external response.*

You can notice changes in:

Face and body language
(e.g., frowning, slouching)

How you talk
(e.g., swearing, soft voice)

Actions
(e.g., Self-Soothe, SIB)

Emotion Name

This is when you put a name on your emotions.

(Notice everything that had to happen to get here!)

After effects

This is what happens in response to your emotions and is how your emotion impacts you in the middle or long term. This can include thoughts, behaviors, memories, body sensations and Secondary Emotions.

SIB = Self-injurious behavior.

The Big Picture of Emotions - An Example

Here is an example of the Big Picture of Emotions.

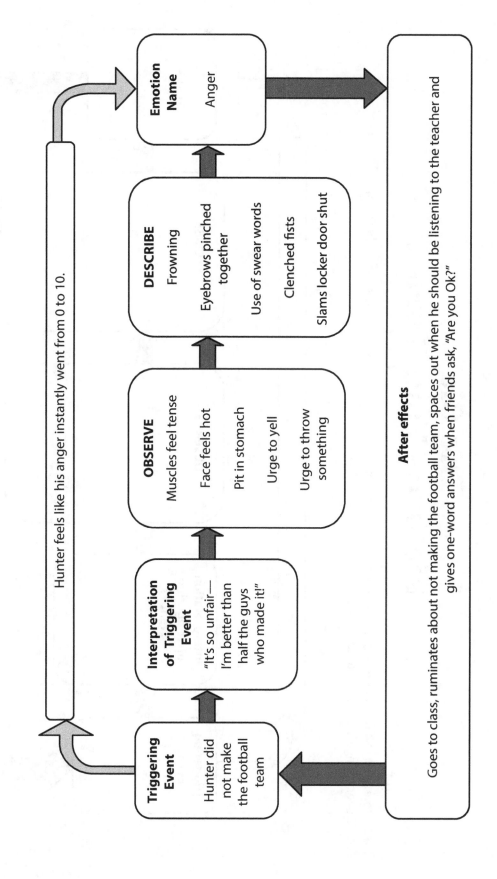

Hunter feels like his anger instantly went from 0 to 10.

Triggering Event

Hunter did not make the football team

Interpretation of Triggering Event

"It's so unfair—I'm better than half the guys who made it!"

OBSERVE

Muscles feel tense

Face feels hot

Pit in stomach

Urge to yell

Urge to throw something

DESCRIBE

Frowning

Eyebrows pinched together

Use of swear words

Clenched fists

Slams locker door shut

Emotion Name

Anger

After effects

Goes to class, ruminates about not making the football team, spaces out when he should be listening to the teacher and gives one-word answers when friends ask, "Are you Ok?"

The Big
Picture - Your Turn

Take some time to think about a time when you were experiencing an emotion. Fill in the chart to help you notice everything that went into that emotional experience.

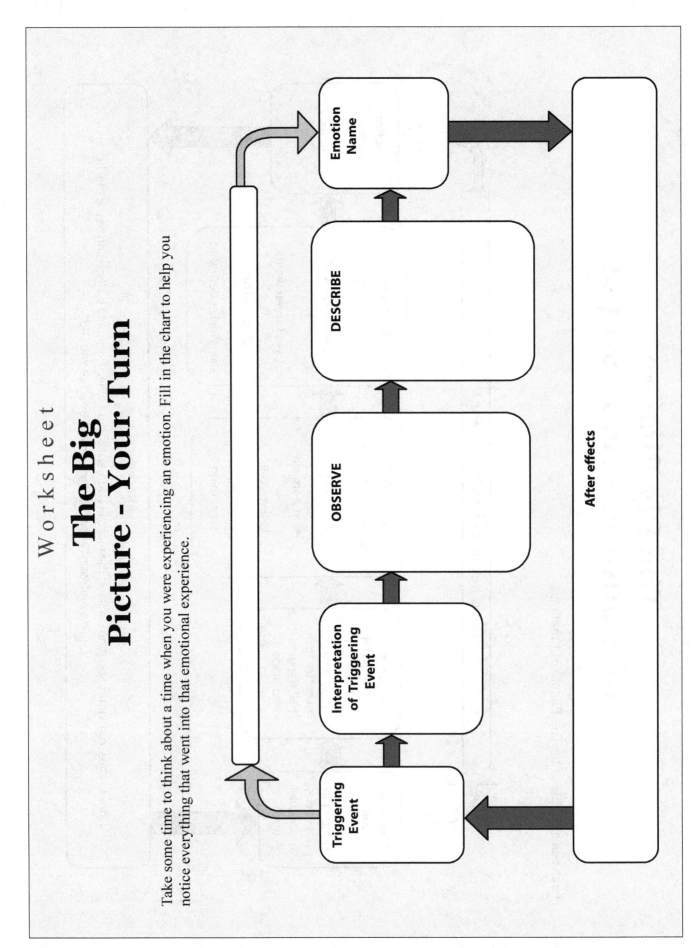

Emotion Name

DESCRIBE

OBSERVE

Interpretation of Triggering Event

Triggering Event

After effects

Be an Emotions Detective

Being aware of your emotions is very important. Knowing how you are feeling will help you:

- Focus on and appreciate enjoyable emotions

- Use skills to manage difficult emotions

- Catch emotions before they get too overwhelming

- Stay in Wise Mind

- _____

- _____

- _____

Learning to be aware of your emotions is like being an Emotions Detective. This means being on the lookout for clues that might help you catch an emotion.

Look for clues in these areas:

Body Sensations: Emotions involve physical changes in the body.

For example: I may have tense muscles and a pounding heart when I feel anxious.

Thoughts: Emotions impact the way we think, including self-talk.

For example: I may say to myself "I can't do it" when feeling depressed.

Communication (Verbal and Nonverbal): Emotions change how we communicate.

For example: I may clench my fists or yell when I feel angry.

Action Urges & Actions: Emotions affect the way we feel like behaving and the way we behave.

For example: I may have urges for self-injurious behavior when feeling guilty, or I may impulsively interrupt others when feeling excited.

Be an Emotions Detective - Your Turn

Use your detective skills to fill in the following worksheet. Keep in mind that this is about you detecting your own emotions, so your clues might be different than other's clues. Remember to review this worksheet occasionally, so you can catch emotions red handed.

Sadness/Depression

Body Sensations:
- *Slowed down*
- • • • • • •

Thoughts:
- *"I can't do anything right."*
- • • • • • •

Communication:
- *Avoid eye contact*
- • • • • • •

Action Urges & Actions:
- *Urge for self-injurious behavior*
- • • • • • •

Anxiety

Body Sensations:
- *Tense muscles*
- • • • • • •

Thoughts:
- *"I'm going crazy."*
- • • • • • •

Communication:
- *Fidgeting*
- • • • • • •

Action Urges & Actions:
- *Urge to skip school*
- • • • • • •

Body Sensations:
- *Face feels hot*
- • • • • • •

Thoughts:
- *"This is so unfair!"*
- • • • • • •

Communication:
- *Yell and curse*
- • • • • • •

Action Urges & Actions:
- *Throw things*
- • • • • • •

Being an emotions detective doesn't just mean noticing difficult emotions, it also means noticing more enjoyable emotions. In fact, in some cases, it can be harder to detect these emotions. Some clues could fit for several emotions. For example, tense muscles can happy for both anxiety and excitement. Make sure to look at all the clues when you are trying to figure out what you are feeling.

Love

Body Sensations:
- Faster heart rate
- _____
- _____
- _____
- _____

Thoughts:
- "He/She is so cute!"
- _____
- _____
- _____

Communication:
- Talk about positives
- _____
- _____
- _____

Action Urges & Actions:
- Urge to text my crush
- _____
- _____
- _____

Happiness

Body Sensations:
- Relaxed muscles
- _____
- _____
- _____

Thoughts:
- "Life is good!"
- _____
- _____

Communication:
- Giggling/laughing
- _____
- _____

Action Urges & Actions:
- Being bouncy or bubbly
- _____
- _____
- _____

Body Sensations:
- Tense muscles
- _____
- _____
- _____

Thoughts:
- "This is so exciting!"
- _____
- _____

Communication:
- Talking about the future
- _____
- _____

Action Urges & Actions:
- Urges to sing or dance
- _____
- _____
- _____

PLEASE

The PLEASE skill is about taking care of your body and physical health. The goal is to reduce *emotional vulnerability* (Linehan, 1993b). When you do not feel well or when you are not taking care of your physical needs, you will are more likely to be emotional and will have a harder time coping with stress.

PL: treat Physical illness

Treating Physical illness means taking care of yourself when you are sick.

• See a doctor when ill   • Take medicines as prescribed   • Get extra sleep when sick

• _____   • _____   • _____

• _____   • _____   • _____

E: balanced Eating

Eat so that you have enough energy to get through the day. Don't eat too much or too little.

• Eat at least one vegetable at every meal   • Only eat sweets as a reward   • Eat mindfully

• Have fruit as a snack after school   • Help make a list of meals for the week   • Learn to cook

• _____   • _____   • _____

• _____   • _____   • _____

A: Avoid mood-altering drugs

Stay away from alcohol and street drugs and only take medications as prescribed. Limit caffeine and avoid tobacco.

• Have one or no sodas/day   • Spend more time with sober friends   • Go to an AA meeting

• Practice assertiveness to say no when offered drugs or alcohol   • Remember the cons of drug use

• _____   • _____

• _____   • _____

S: balanced Sleep

Try to get the right amount of sleep for you. Do not sleep too much or too little. Most people need between 8 and 10 hours of sleep each night.

- Go to bed and wake up at the same time every day
- Make sure your bed is comfortable
- Don't read or watch TV in bed
- Keep naps to a minimum
- Use a Self-Soothe skill before bed

- _____
- _____
- _____

- _____
- _____
- _____

E: balanced Exercise

Try to get at least 20 minutes of exercise every day. Remember to stay physically active.

- Take the stairs instead of the elevator
- Take a short walk every day
- Join a sports team
- Ask a friend to go to the gym
- Help with yard work
- Shovel snow in winter

- _____
- _____
- _____

- _____
- _____
- _____

My PLEASE Evaluation

Fill in this worksheet to help you identify your strengths and areas for growth with the PLEASE skill.

	What I do well . . .	What I need to work on ...	Barriers	Solutions
treat **P**hysica**L** illness				
balanced **E**ating				
Avoid mood-altering drugs				
balanced **S**leep				
balanced **E**xercise				

Build Mastery

Build Mastery means doing something that helps you feel *confident*, *capable* and *in control* (Linehan, 1993b).

It is easy to over-focus on things you see as weaknesses or failures, and over-focusing on these areas will lead you to feel insecure and self-conscious. Build Mastery counteracts these feelings by helping you to focus on activities that create feelings of accomplishment.

You can Build Mastery by doing daily chores and tasks:

- Take a shower
- Do your makeup
- Clean your room
- Get homework done
- Study for a test

- _____
- _____
- _____

You can also Build Mastery by doing things you are already good at, or by working on a new goal:

- Go for a run
- Work on a craft project
- Write poetry
- Doodle or draw
- Practice piano
- Talk to someone new at school
- Use DBT skills instead of engaging in self-injurious behavior
- Work on assertiveness by saying no

- _____
- _____
- _____
- _____
- _____
- _____

It is important to Build Mastery every day.

Just Act

You have probably had the experience of telling yourself, "I'll get this done today," and at the end of the day, the task is still not done. Often we think about accomplishing something but do not put our thought into action. The Just Act skill is about putting your good intentions into action.

Many things can get in the way of acting:

- You might get busy or distracted.

- You might talk yourself out of it or find excuses not to act.

- You might be used to being a certain way, and it can be scary and hard to do something new.

- _____

- _____

Use the Just Act skill to overcome these barriers so that you can accomplish a task or goal.

Use Just Act is to give yourself only a small amount of time to mindfully think about getting something done—but then it's time to stop thinking and start acting.

When you use Just Act, do not let yourself procrastinate or talk yourself out of an effective action.

Take a look at this example:

Katie recently joined an exercise class. The first two times she went, she really enjoyed herself and noticed feeling a bit brighter the day after. Last week, however, Katie was lying on the couch thinking about going to her exercise class. She went back and forth in her mind, thinking, "It's so cold out tonight. I know I had fun last time, but it wouldn't be a big deal if I skipped once. Besides, I could do my homework instead." Katie didn't go to her exercise class and also did not get her homework done. At school the next day, her friends told her how much fun they had at class, and Katie regretted not going.

This week, Katie is having the same mental debate about going to her exercise class, only this time, she used Just Act. Katie noticed her thoughts about skipping and decided, "I'm just going to go!" She got off the couch, grabbed her gym bag and headed out. At class, Katie had a blast with her friends and felt good about herself for the rest of the day.

Use Just Act to bring your good intentions to life and get things done.

Give Myself Credit

The Give Myself Credit skill is about being mindful of and appreciating your efforts or work toward a goal.

Achieving a goal can be a long process and requires a lot of small steps.

This means that progress may be slow, and it can be easy to get discouraged.

The Give Myself Credit skill helps us to deal with this process by focusing on how far we have come, rather than focusing on how far we have to go.

To use the Give Myself Credit skill, notice and appreciate every small step.

Remember that you do not need to have your goal accomplished or even to see change to use Give Myself Credit. Instead, Give Myself Credit is about celebrating every step—even if that step didn't go like you wanted it to.

Give Myself Credit will help you be motivated and ready to take the next step and keep trying.

Here are some examples of Give Myself Credit:

- "I did my best!"
- "I'm proud of myself for trying something new."
- "I followed through and took a step."
- _____
- _____
- _____

Use the Give Myself Credit skill every time you Build Mastery.

My "Way to Go!" List

This worksheet will help you keep track of how you Build Mastery and help you Practice Give Myself Credit. It can be easy to over-focus on what you did *not* do, so this list will help you find balance by reminding yourself to notice all the things you *have* accomplished. Remember that even small steps count.

Take credit for all the small steps you took and give yourself a "Way to go!"

Date	How I Used Build Mastery Today
October 28	Got up early to get ready for the day Raised my hand in class Used Self-Soothe when I felt anxious

Build Positive Experiences

The Build Positive Experiences skill means doing something that is pleasurable and fun (Linehan, 1993b). Build Positive Experiences will help you balance difficult emotions by having fun and feeling fulfilled.

There are several ways to Build Positive Experiences:

Notice positive events that are already happening. It can be easy to miss positives events that happen every day. It is important to be on the lookout for these positive events, no matter how small. Here are some examples:

- Notice the sun shining and what it feels like on your skin.

- Notice how it feels to talk with a friend at school.

- Pay attention to how you feel watching a favorite TV show.

Short-term Positive Experiences. Short-term Positive Experiences are things that you can do <u>right now</u> to feel good (Linehan, 1993b). These experiences can be spontaneous or may require a little planning. Here are some examples:

- Watch a funny video on YouTube.

- Text a friend.

- Make a scrapbook.

- Plan a party.

Long-term Positive Experiences. Long-term Positive Experiences are positive experiences that require a lot of planning and are accomplished through many smaller steps (Linehan, 1993b). They can be life goals or can be bigger changes that help you build a life you are excited to live. Here are some examples:

- Learn karate.

- Get good grades.

- Learn to speak Spanish.

It is important to create both short- and long-term Positive Experiences.

Remember to use Mindfulness skills with your Positive Experiences. Notice when your attention goes to stressors, worries or negative thoughts and then bring your attention back to your Positive Experience. Give yourself permission to have fun and only focus on your Positive Experience.

100 Ways to Build Positive Experiences

Help fill in the blanks to create a list of 100 Ways to Build Positive Experiences.
Remember to include short- and long-term Positive Experiences!

1. Take a bubble bath
2. Watch videos on YouTube®
3. Go to a movie
4. Plan a date
5. Listen to music
6. Post something on social media
7. Write a song
8. Look at colleges
9. Play a sport
10. Think about a favorite place
11. Play video games
12. Organize your room
13. Go skateboarding
14. Plan your wedding
15. Bake cookies
16. Imagine accomplishing your goals
17. Go to the zoo

18. Journal
19. Eat ice cream
20. Go bike riding
21. Paint a picture
22. Read about possible careers
23. Take pictures
24. Join an after school club
25. Go for a run
26. Daydream
27. Take driver's ed classes
28. Read a book
29. Plan your dress and hair for prom
30. Work on cars
31. Meditate
32. Pray
33. Take acting classes
34. Light a candle

35. Text a friend
36. Learn to play the guitar
37. Do a puzzle
38. Take a walk
39. Go to the mall
40. Play a game on your phone
41. Think about your accomplishments
42. Go to a concert
43. Think about how to get good grades
44. Read meaningful old letters or emails
45. Volunteer
46. Write poetry
47. Make a collage
48. Go swimming
49. Watch a movie on Netflix™
50. Do your nails
51. Play a board game with your friends

52. Go on a camping trip
53. Apply for jobs
54. Read your favorite magazine
55. Spend time with your pet
56. Make a scrapbook
57. Invite your friends to sleep over
58. Plan and go on a picnic
59. Take a dance class
60. Go to a youth group at church
61. Look at old photos
62. Pack a special lunch to have at school
63. Go to your school's football game
64. Go bowling
65. Learn how to knit
66. Go to the beach
67. Learn to cook a new meal
68. Spend time with family

69. Go the library
70. Go to a museum (e.g., art, science)
71. Do yoga
72. Form a band
73. Learn a new hobby
74. Call an old friend
75. _____
76. _____
77. _____
78. _____
79. _____
80. _____
81. _____
82. _____
83. _____
84. _____
85. _____

86. _____
87. _____
88. _____
89. _____
90. _____
91. _____
92. _____
93. _____
94. _____
95. _____
96. _____
97. _____
98. _____
99. _____
100. _____

Opposite to Emotion

Emotions love themselves (Linehan, 1993b). This means that when you are feeling an emotion, you will have urges and thoughts that keep that emotion around. Here is an example:

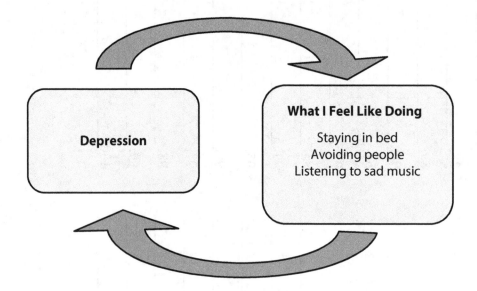

Acting Opposite to Emotion means doing the opposite of what you feel like doing (Linehan, 1993b). This will help to break out of an emotion and create a new emotion. Here is an example:

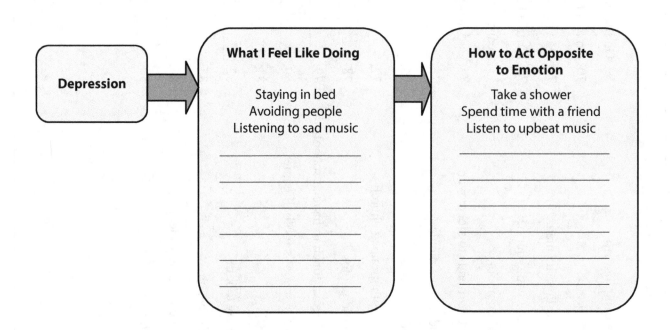

Remember, you won't feel like doing the opposite, but acting Opposite to Emotion will help you to break out of the cycle that keeps difficult emotions around.

Worksheet
Opposite to Emotion – Your Turn

Take a look at ways to act Opposite to Emotion with several other emotions:

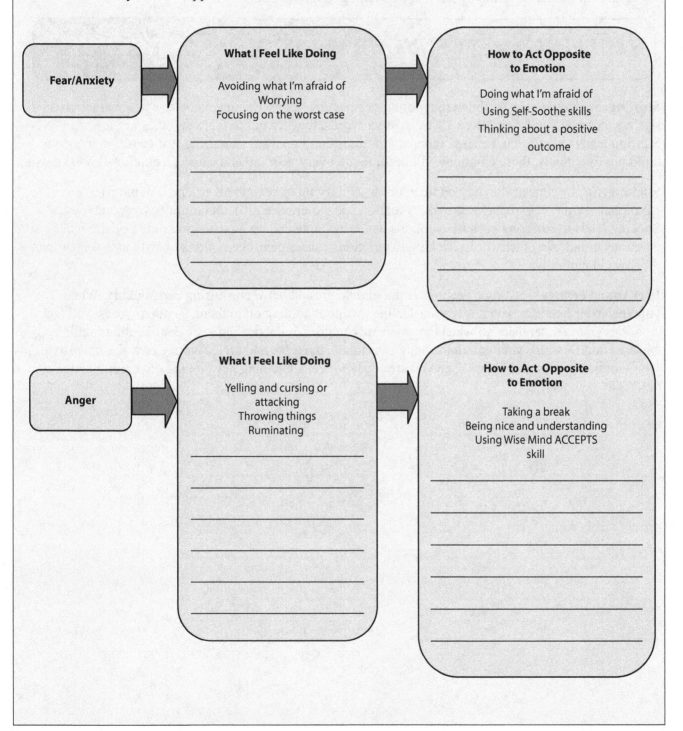

Feel Your Feelings

The Feel Your Feelings skill is about being mindful of your emotions. This means noticing and experiencing your emotions and letting them naturally come and go (Linehan, 1993b).

Feel Your Feelings sometimes means experiencing painful emotions without turning the painful emotions into suffering.

We create emotional suffering by stuffing or sticking to our emotions.

STUFFING	FEEL YOUR FEELINGS	STICKING

Stuffing. *Stuffing* means bottling up, ignoring or rejecting your emotions. People who are emotional stuffers try to push their emotions away. In other words, they try not to feel what they are feeling. Stuffing leads to suffering, because ignored emotions don't go away—stuffing just causes emotions to build up. Eventually, those emotions will become too overwhelming and cause an emotional breakdown.

Sticking. *Sticking* means holding on to emotions and trying to keep them around. People who are emotional stickers will replay a stressful situation and experience difficult emotions over and over. Sticking leads to suffering because emotions naturally come and go, but sticking does not allow the emotions to fade. In other words, sticking to emotions causes painful emotions to last much longer than they would naturally.

Feel Your Feelings. Feel Your Feelings is the middle ground between stuffing and sticking. When you Feel Your Feelings, you notice your feelings without holding on to them. In other words, you feel emotions and then let them go when they are ready to go. To practice the Feel Your Feelings skill, Observe and Describe your emotions, body sensations, thoughts and urges. Notice how the intensity of your emotion comes and goes. When you are ready to feel something new, let the old emotion go and notice the new feeling.

Feel Your Feelings Evaluation

Are you an emotional stuffer or an emotional sticker? Are you good at Feeling Your Feelings? Look at the lists below and check the items that fit for you. If you check a lot in the stuffing or sticking category, it might be helpful to focus on skills that help you Feel Your Feelings.

Stuffing:

☐ I frequently pretend like everything is Ok when it is not.

☐ I ignore my emotions.

☐ I smile even when I'm sad, hurt, anxious or angry.

☐ People are surprised when they find out I'm depressed or anxious.

☐ I focus on other people's problems and ignore my own.

☐ I feel emotionally numb a lot.

☐ I will hold in my emotions until they are too big to ignore.

☐ People tell me I'm emotionally distant.

☐ _____

☐ _____

☐ _____

Sticking:

☐ I often replay a crisis or difficult event over and over in my head.

☐ I focus a lot on my difficult emotions.

☐ I beat myself up a lot for things that are far in the past.

☐ Most of the time I don't let myself see the positives.

☐ People tell me I don't get over things very easily.

☐ People tell me I make a bigger deal than I should out of things.

☐ It's hard for me to let go of difficult emotions.

☐ _____

☐ _____

☐ _____

Feel My Feelings:

☐ I notice my enjoyable and difficult feelings when they are happening.

☐ I let my feelings come and go.

☐ I notice both the positives and negatives.

☐ I am usually able to tell people how I'm feeling.

☐ I am comfortable with my emotions.

☐ The people close to me usually know how I'm feeling.

☐ When I have a difficult emotion, I can feel it without holding onto it.

☐ _____

☐ _____

☐ _____

Emotion Regulation Module Skills List

The Emotion Regulation module is about learning to *understand and balance your emotions.*

PL	PLEASE	Take care of your physical health, self-care.
BM	Build Mastery	Do what helps you to feel confident, capable, in control.
JA	Just Act	Be active and get a task done.
GMC	Give Myself Credit	Focus on your accomplishments.
BPE	Build Positive Experiences	Do things that create enjoyable emotions; have fun.
O2E	Opposite to Emotion	Do the opposite of urges from difficult emotions.
FYF	Feel Your Feelings	Let your emotions naturally come and go.

Interpersonal Effectiveness Module

The Interpersonal Effectiveness module teaches skills to improve relationships. The Interpersonal Effectiveness module has three goals to help you (Linehan, 1993b):

- Build and keep healthy relationships.

- Make requests and say no.

- Feel good about yourself in relationships.

Let's take a closer look at each goal.

Build and Keep Healthy Relationships

You can build and keep healthy relationships by acting in ways that make it more likely for the other person to enjoy time with you and feel invested in your relationship (Linehan, 1993b).

The focus with the first goal is the *other person*.

A question that helps you focus on this goal is: "How do I want the other person to feel about me/our relationship after this interaction (Linehan, 1993b)?"

The skill goes that with this goal is GIVE.

Make Requests and Say No

This goal is about learning to be assertive. Assertiveness helps you ask for what you want and makes it more likely that you will get your wants and needs met in relationships (Linehan, 1993b). Assertiveness will also help you say no.

The focus with this goal is your *objectives* (or what you want).

A question that helps you focus on this goal is: "What do I want to change after this interaction (Linehan, 1993b)?"

The skill that goes with this goal is DEAR MAN.

Feel Good About Yourself in Relationships

This goal is about respecting your own values and beliefs and acting in ways that will help you feel capable and effective in relationships (Linehan, 1993b).

The focus with this goal is *you*.

A question that helps you focus on this goal is: "How do I want to feel about myself after this interaction (Linehan, 1993b)?"

The skill that goes with this goal is FAST.

My Relationships Evaluation

Before we dive into the Interpersonal Effectiveness module, take a moment to complete this Relationship Evaluation. Think about significant people in your life and identify strengths and areas for growth for each relationship.

Fill in the first three columns in each section. Leave the last column blank. You will return to fill in this column after you have learned the Interpersonal Effectiveness skills.

Family

Name	What is working in this relationship?	How can this relationship improve?	How can you use Interpersonal Effectiveness skills in this relationship?

Non-Family Adults (Teachers, Pastors, etc.)

Name	What is working in this relationship?	How can this relationship improve?	How can you use Interpersonal Effectiveness skills in this relationship?

Friends

Name	What is working in this relationship?	How can this relationship improve?	How can you use Interpersonal Effectiveness skills in this relationship?

Peers

Name	What is working in this relationship?	How can this relationship improve?	How can you use Interpersonal Effectiveness skills in this relationship?

Other Relationships

Name	What is working in this relationship?	How can this relationship improve?	How can you use Interpersonal Effectiveness skills in this relationship?

My Relationship With Myself

My name	What is working in your relationship with yourself?	How can you improve your relationship with yourself?	How can you use Interpersonal Effectiveness skills to improve your relationship with yourself?

What Do You Believe About Relationships?

It is common for people to have beliefs about relationships that are not true. Our beliefs impact how we act in relationships. Sometimes how we see relationships can be ineffective and can create conflict or poor self-respect in relationships. This is why it is important to examine your beliefs. Take a look at this list of misconceptions about relationships. Check the ones that fit for you.

☐ I can't deal with other people being upset with me.

☐ I don't deserve to get what I want or need in relationships.

☐ If I ask for help, people will see me as weak.

☐ I would be selfish if I said no.

☐ It's my fault when people around me are upset.

☐ I can't be Ok if people around me are not Ok.

☐ If other people are upset, it's because I've done or said something wrong.

☐ I always have to agree with other people, or I won't fit in.

☐ I have to yell and get angry for people to take me seriously.

☐ To be a good person, I should always put other people first.

☐ Other people's needs and wants are more important than my needs and wants.

☐ There is no way I can handle conflict.

☐ Other people can make my decisions better than I can.

☐ My needs and wants should come first.

☐ _____

☐ _____

☐ _____

Take a look at the next worksheet, "Interpersonal Skills: The Basics," to learn more about why statements on this list are untrue.

Interpersonal Skills: The Basics

Interpersonal Effectiveness skills are not about the outcome. Using Interpersonal Effectiveness skills is tricky, because these skills involve other people and we cannot control what others do. Using these skills makes getting the outcome we want *more likely,* but we only have control over our part of the relationship. This means that when we use Interpersonal Effectiveness skills, we may not get the outcome we want. It is important to give yourself credit for using skills, and not let the outcome determine if you are successful.

Interpersonal Effectiveness skills can be used for my relationship with myself. In*ter*personal skills can also be used as In*tra*personal skills. *Intrapersonal* means the way you communicate with yourself. The longest and closest relationship you will have in your life is the relationship that you have with yourself, so it is important to attend to this relationship. Interpersonal skills can be used with other people but can also apply to the relationship that you have with yourself.

It's Ok and normal to have needs and wants. Everyone has needs and wants, and this is Ok and normal (Linehan, 1993b). You have the right to ask for what you need or want from others, and it is Ok to say no to others so that you can meet your own needs and wants. You can assert yourself and still be a good person.

I have the right to say no. Saying no can be difficult and scary. Even though it can be difficult, you have the right to say no if you want or need to. You may want to please people that you care about, but you do not have to please them all the time (Linehan, 1993b). Sometimes you will need to say no so that you can take care of yourself. You are just as important as everyone else. If someone gets upset with you for saying no, that does not mean that you should have said yes.

It's Ok to be different from others. It's Ok to have your own interests and likes, even if they are different from those of your friends or people around you. It is normal to want to fit in, but remember to be yourself, too.

Balance Independence & Support

It is common for teenagers not to see eye to eye with their parents. Finding balance between independence and support is one way the relationship with your parents can be difficult.

| INDEPENDENCE | BALANCE | SUPPORT |

Independence. It's normal for teenagers to want independence. With independence, you can do things and go places on your own. You may also want privacy and not want to talk to your parents about your thoughts or feelings. Independence is helpful because you learn to do new things and start figuring out who you are away from your parents.

Having too much independence can create problems, because without rules and limits, you could get into trouble. Too much independence can also cause you to feel alone and unsupported. Your independence can be difficult and scary for your parents. Some parents are used to being supportive and having more "say" in what you do. These parents may want to be involved in your decisions. Other parents notice your abilities to do things on your own and give you too much independence. These parents may have adult-like expectations of you.

Support. Although teenagers want more independence, your parents' support is also needed. Support is helpful because you know someone is looking out for you, and having your parents make decisions about some things can make life less overwhelming. Support can also mean having limits and boundaries so that you don't take on more than you are ready for.

Having too much support can be a problem. Too much support could feel suffocating, and if you don't have some freedom, you won't be able to learn from your mistakes and gain new skills. Too much support might also prevent you from figuring out who you are as a person. Parents might give you too much support because they are afraid of you making mistakes. Parents may not give you enough support because they are busy with other things or because they think you can handle more than you are ready for.

Balance. When you have balance between independence and support, you are able to try new things, have some freedom to make your own choices *and* have support with and limits on what you take on yourself. When you have both independence *and* support, you are working together with your parents. This will help you and them feel more comfortable and allow you to get what you need.

Take a look at the next worksheet, "Independence and Support Evaluation," to figure out how you and your parents can achieve a balance between independence and support.

Independence & Support Evaluation

It can be a difficult to find balance with independence and support in your relationships with your parents. This evaluation will help you figure out what you need to work toward this balance. Complete this worksheet and discuss your ideas with your parents.

Independence—What things do you think you can do independently?

Home (examples: I can chose my own bedtime; I can be responsible for my own laundry)
School (examples: I can keep track of my assignments; I can ask the teacher for help if I need it)
Friends/Peers (examples: I can arrange plans with friends; I can set limits with peers if I need to)
Other Areas:

Support—How can your parents support you? What limits do your parents need to set?

Home (examples: My parents can help me with safety by checking on me at night; I am Ok with reminders to clean)
School (examples: I'd like reminders of due dates for assignments and homework help)
Friends/Peers (examples: My parents can meet my friends and know where I am going)
Other Areas:

Balance Priorities & Demands

There are many ways that relationships can be difficult. One type of difficult situation is finding balance between priorities and demands.

PRIORITIES	BALANCE	DEMANDS

Priorities. Priorities are things that are important to you and on which you want to spend your time (Linehan, 1993b). Priorities help you develop hobbies, interests and your own sense of self.

> Example: It's important to Jake to play video games to unwind after school.

If your time is only spent on your priorities, others may feel angry, neglected or unimportant, and this could strain your relationships.

> Example: If Jake ignores his mom's requests for him to do his chores and instead spends all his time on video games, his mom will probably get angry, and this could lead to fights.

Demands. Demands are things that are important to others and are what they want you to spend your time on (Linehan, 1993b). Demands are a natural part of relationships. Other people have expectations of you and your time.

> Example: It's important to Jake's mom that Jake gets his chores done.

If your time is only spent on demands, you may feel overwhelmed and stressed and will likely become resentful of others.

> Example: If Jake spends all his time on chores and does not take a break to play video games to unwind, he will probably feel burned out and overwhelmed, and this could also lead to fights with his mom.

Balance. Finding a balance between priorities and demands is really important. With this balance, you and others will get what you need in the relationship.

> Example: If Jake spends some of his time on video games *and* some of his time on chores, both he and his mom will get what they need and will be less likely to get into fights.

Ways to Practice Interpersonal Effectiveness Skills

Interpersonal Effectiveness skills are best learned through lots of practice. Often we need these skills when we are in intense situations where we have strong emotions. This is why it is important to first practice Interpersonal Effectiveness skills in situations where we do not have strong emotions. This will help us get used to the skills without the pressure of a difficult situation. Here are some ways to practice these skills. Add your own, too!

1. Ask a sibling or friend to borrow something.

2. Invite a neighbor or classmate over.

3. Ask to sit with a new group of people at lunch.

4. Raise your hand and answer a question in class.

5. When out to dinner with your family, order your own food.

6. Say hi to a classmate to whom you have not talked before.

7. Ask a teacher a question after class.

8. Ask a classmate for help with an assignment.

9. Offer to help your mom or dad with a chore at home.

10. Call to make an appointment for a haircut.

11. Go to a store and ask a sales associate to help you find something.

12. Say no to a request that a friend makes.

13. Ask a friend for a small favor (such as giving you ride to school or lending you money for a soda)

14. Disagree with someone's opinion.

15. Give your mom or dad a compliment.

16. _____

17. _____

18. _____

19. _____

20. _____

Attend To Relationships

Attend to Relationships is a skill we use to pay attention to and care for our relationships. Having relationships is sort of like having a garden. Plants are more likely to grow and bloom if you notice and care for them, just as relationships are likely to be effective and healthy if you care for them. Following are some ways to Attend to Relationships.

Talk to and spend time with others regularly.

- Spending time together will help you feel comfortable around each other.

- Time together will help strengthen your bond.

- Having shared experiences will help you create memories.

- _____

- _____

Don't let problems build up (Linehan, 1993b).

- When there is a problem, address it and don't let it build up.

- Resentment hurts relationships.

- By talking through a problem, you can avoid carrying around built-up emotions.

- Resolve a conflict before it gets too big and overwhelming.

- _____

- _____

Use your skills to avoid problems (Linehan, 1993b).

- Be mindful of and respect others' boundaries.

- Assert yourself if someone crosses your boundaries.

- _____

- _____

Balance sharing with listening.

- Share your own thoughts, opinions and emotions. Let the other person get to know you and be active in conversations.

- Let the other person speak, and listen mindfully. Avoid judgments, even if you disagree. Use active listening by reflecting what you hear the other person saying.

- _____

- _____

GIVE

The goal of the GIVE skill is to build and keep healthy relationships.

With this skill, we are considering how we want the other person to feel about us and the relationship (Linehan, 1993b). Each letter in GIVE stands for a way that we can build and keep healthy relationships.

G—be Gentle

Being Gentle means being kind and respectful. Here are ways we can be Gentle:

- Use a soft tone of voice
- Make eye contact
- Use a Non-Judgmental Stance
- Give a compliment
- Listen
- Give caring feedback

- _____
- _____
- _____

- _____
- _____
- _____

Being Gentle is important when things are going well *and* when things are not going well in relationships. Here are some ways to be Gentle when you are fighting or have hit a rough spot in your relationship:

- Do not call names
- Do not use physical aggression
- Do not use swear
- Do not yell
- Do not threaten to leave
- Do not threaten to hurt yourself
- Do not use guilt trips
- Do not use put-downs
- Hear the other person out
- Take a break if you are in Emotion Mind

- _____
- _____

- _____
- _____

I—act Interested

Acting Interested helps the other person feel valued and important. Here are ways to act Interested:

- Actively listen
- Do not interrupt
- Ask questions
- Make good eye contact
- Have open body language
- Be patient
- Ask, "How are you?"
- Be sensitive to others' opinions/wants/emotions

- _____
- _____
- _____

- _____
- _____
- _____

V—Validate

To Validate means to show that you understand the other person's opinions, feelings, behaviors, wants or point of view. Validation is simply acknowledgment of the other person. The goal of Validation is to express an understanding.

Validation does NOT mean that you agree, approve of or like the other person's opinions, feelings, behaviors, wants or point of view.

Validation is important because it:

- Helps the other person feel heard and understood

- Builds trust and respect in relationships

- Helps people feel less angry during a conflict

- Helps you work together to resolve a problem

- _____

- _____

Validation involves active listening: This means hearing what someone says and then sharing how you heard what was said. Here are some examples of how to validate:

- "Considering what you have been through, it makes sense for you to feel this way."

- "So you are angry because _____."

- "I can see why you feel the way you do."

- "It sounds like _____."

- "I can understand why you see it that way."

- _____

- _____

- _____

When you Validate, DO NOT:

- Use BUT or HOWEVER in your validation. Doing this causes the other person to miss your validation because he or she is focused on what you said after the "but."

- Personalize, which means sharing your own emotions or a time when you went through something similar. Doing this makes it about you. Remember the goal of Validation is to share an understanding of the other person.

E—Easy Manner

Having an Easy Manner means being easy going, and not taking things too seriously. Having an Easy Manner will help other people feel relaxed and comfortable. Having an Easy Manner does NOT mean that you take nothing seriously. Use your Wise Mind to help you decide when it is important to be relaxed and lighthearted. Here are some ways to have an Easy Manner:

- Make a joke
- Smile
- Focus on the positives

- Let little things go
- Be polite
- Make small talk

- _____
- _____
- _____

- _____
- _____
- _____

Validation

Validation means simply *expressing an understanding* of the other person. When we Validate, we listen and reflect back what we heard or tell someone how we understand his or her point of view or feelings. Consider relationships that you think need Validation. Be mindful about Validating over the next week. Make sure to use Validation at least once.

Answer the following questions about your use of Validation:

What was the situation? _____

_____

_____

_____

_____

_____

Who did you Validate? _____

What did you say as Validation? _____

_____

_____

_____

What did you notice about how Validation impacted the other person or the relationship?

_____

_____

_____

_____

_____

DEAR MAN

DEAR MAN is an assertiveness skill. Assertiveness means directly and clearly making a request or saying no. The goal is to ask another person to do something or to say no to another person's request (Linehan, 1993b). Each letter in DEAR MAN stands for a way that we can be assertive.

D—Describe

- Share the facts about the current situation.
- Starting with the facts will get you and the other person on the same page.

    For example: "I called you last night, and you never called me back."

E—Express

- Express your feelings and opinions about the facts.
- Remember to label feelings as feelings and opinions as opinions.
- Try to be Non-Judgmental and avoid attacking or blaming.
- "I" statements will help you express. Start a sentence with "I" and remember not to blame the other person for your feelings.

    For example, instead of saying, "You made me angry," say, "I felt angry when you did not call me back."

A—Assert

- Ask for what you want or say no clearly and directly.
- Do not assume that the other person already knows what you want.

    For example: "Will you please call me back?"

R—Reinforce

Reinforce means doing something that makes what you want more likely. There are several ways to Reinforce:

- Share the *positive impacts* of the other person doing what you ask.

    For example: "I feel important and happy when you call me back."

- Share the *negative impacts* of the other person doing what you ask. (Often, it's more helpful to start with the positive impacts and only share the negative impacts for things you need.)

For example: "I care about our relationship less when I don't hear from you."

• Offer the other person a *reward* for doing what you ask. Sometimes rewards can simply be saying thank you and acting grateful. Sometimes rewards can be doing something in return.

For example: "I will make you a friendship bracelet if you try to call back more."

M—Mindful

• Stay focused on your goal. Remember why you are using DEAR MAN.

• Do not get distracted, and always come back to your goal.

• Several techniques will help you be mindful:

Broken Record
• Keep asking or saying no—over and over again.

• Sometimes being a Broken Record means repeating yourself in the same conversation, and sometimes it means repeating yourself in several separate conversations.

Ignore
• Pay attention to and ignore attempts to change the subject, threats or comments that are meant to distract you.

• Do not respond to comments unless they have to do with your goal for DEAR MAN.

Take a Break
• Sometimes difficult conversations can trigger Emotion Mind.

• Notice if you or the other person is in Emotion Mind and take a break.

• Remember, you can always come back to the conversation later.

A—Act confident

• You might not always feel confident when asserting yourself, but Acting confident can make DEAR MAN more effective.

• Here are some ways to Act confident:

Make eye contact	Speak clearly	Have straight posture
Do not talk too fast	Think encouraging thoughts	Do not mumble
_____	_____	_____
_____	_____	_____

N—Negotiate

- Compromise, or be willing to give in on some things, so you can get some of what you want.

- Offer alternative options.

    For example: "Instead of calling, you could send me a short text."

- Be willing to work with the other person.

    Turn the Tables
    - If the other person keeps saying no to your requests or is unwilling to negotiate, put him or her in charge of figuring out a solution.

    - Ask, "What do you think we should do?" or "How do you think we can solve this problem?"

DEAR MAN Example

Take a look at this example to get a better idea of what it looks like to use the DEAR MAN skill.

Hannah is working hard learning DBT skills so she can stop using self-injury as a way to cope. Her best friend Emma also struggles with self-injury, but is not learning DBT. Although Emma knows she should work on her self-injury, she is not ready to change. Hannah wants to stay friends with Emma, but Hannah gets triggered every time Emma talks about her self-injury.

Hannah uses DEAR MAN to ask Emma not to talk about self-injury. Take a look at how the conversation went, and then answer the questions that follow:

Hannah: "Emma, when you told me about your self-injury yesterday I got triggered to do self-injury myself. It's really frustrating."

Emma: "I'm sorry, I feel so bad! It's just that we've always talked about everything together."

Hannah: "You are my best friend, and I love being able to talk with you about anything, but, I'm working hard on not doing self-injury, and it's hard to deal with being triggered."

Emma: "Well, I don't want to bring you down like that. I am such a bad friend."

Hannah: "You are my best friend, and I love spending time with you. Can we just make it a rule not talk about our self-injury with each other?"

Emma: "But what if I really need someone to talk to about it? You know I don't have anyone else."

Hannah: "I can talk to you about some of the skills that I'm learning to deal with self injury, but I don't want to know details about your self-injury—it just makes it too hard for me to stop my own."

Emma: "But what if I really just need to vent about it?"

Hannah: "Maybe you could write it in a journal. I've done that and it really helps."

Emma: "I suppose I could try that."

Hannah: "Thank you, and I do still want to spend time together. If we don't talk about self-injury, I'll be less stressed when we are together."

Emma: "I guess I get that. I can try."

Look at the different skills in DEAR MAN and write down how Hannah used each skill:

Describe Share the facts of the current situation	
Express Share your emotions and opinions about the facts	
Assert Ask for what you want	
Reinforce Do something to make what you want more likely (share the positive or negative impacts, offer a reward)	
Mindful Don't get distracted—focus on your goal	
Appear confident Look strong and self-assured	
Negotiate Compromise—find a solution that works for both people	

DEAR MAN Practice

Complete this worksheet to help you prepare DEAR MAN. Planning DEAR MAN will help you be prepared to ask for what you want or to say no.

Think of a situation in which you want to assert yourself.

Describe the situation:
What is your objective (what do you want from the other person)?
D—DESCRIBE: What are the facts of the current situation?
E—EXPRESS: What are your opinions and emotions about the facts?
A—ASSERT: Ask for what you want.
R—REINFORCE: What can you give or take away to help you get what you want?

M—MINDFUL: How can you stay focused on your objective?

A—APPEAR CONFIDENT: How can you look confident and self-assured?

N—NEGOTIATE: How can you compromise to still get some of what you want?

DEAR MAN Evaluation

After trying DEAR MAN, answer these questions to help you to reflect on how it went.

What went well with **DEAR MAN**?

What did not go well with **DEAR MAN**?

What would be helpful next time you do **DEAR MAN**?

FAST

It is important to like yourself and the way that you act with others. The FAST skill helps teach you to act in ways that increase your self-respect in relationships (Linehan, 1993b).

F—Fair. Being Fair means balancing your wants and needs with those of the other person. In other words, when you are Fair, you are remembering to consider yourself and the other person.

Here are some examples of ways to be Fair:

- Accept responsibility for your own mistakes
- Be kind when others make mistakes
- Do not blame others for your emotions

- _____
- _____

- Take turns deciding what to do
- Take turns giving and taking
- Take turns calling or texting

- _____
- _____

A—no Apologies. No Apologies means not _over-apologizing_. In other words, do not apologize for things that are not your fault or for accidents. When you say, "I'm sorry," you send yourself the message, "I'm wrong." Giving yourself this message over and over again can wear down your self-respect. This is why it is important to be mindful of apologizing.

Here are some examples what _not_ to apologize for:

- Your needs or wants
- Your emotions
- Your decisions

- Saying no
- Other people's actions
- Your opinions

- Making a request
- Other people's emotions
- Being successful

- _____
- _____

- _____
- _____

- _____
- _____

Here are some examples of what to say instead of "I'm sorry":

- "I wish that things were different."
- "I know this is hard for you."
- "Excuse me."
- "I understand why you are upset."

- Use validation to express an understanding of another point of view.

- _____
- _____
- _____

- _____
- _____
- _____

S—Stick to your values. Values are things or beliefs that are important to you. Sometimes we can be out of touch with our values. This is why it is important to take some time and think about what is important to you.

Here are some examples of values. Circle the ones that you value, and add your own:

• Family	• Education	• Sports	• Health	• Fun	• Money
• Spirituality	• Religion	• Adventure	• Safety	• Freedom	• Good grades
• Friends	• Animals	• Love	• Romance	• Charity	• Individuality
• Peace	• Honesty	• Hard work	• Beauty	• Technology	• Accomplishment
• Privacy	• Openness	• Rules	• Science	• Cleanliness	• Clothes/fashion
• Creativity	• Sobriety	• Career	• Art	• Music	• Being a leader
• Kindness	• Teamwork	• Trust	• Downtime	• Knowledge	• Responsibility

• _____   • _____   • _____

• _____   • _____   • _____

• _____   • _____   • _____

• _____   • _____   • _____

Stick to your values means that you act in ways that match your values. This means spending time on what is important to you. For example, if family is important to you, you can Stick to values by having family time every week.

Stick to values also means not giving up what is important to you for what is important to someone else. Giving up your values can cause you to lose self-respect. Remember your own values in relationships. Take a look at the next page to learn more about yourself and your values.

T—Truthful. Being Truthful means doing your best to tell the truth and avoid being dishonest. Even though it can be difficult to be honest, you will feel better about yourself if you tell the truth.

Here are some ways to be Truthful:

• Do not act helpless when you are not.

• Say "I don't know" instead of lying.

• Use self-soothe when it is hard to be honest.

• Admit to mistakes.

• Do not exaggerate.

• Do not leave details out on purpose.

• _____   • _____

• _____   • _____

Self-Evaluation

The FAST skill is about increasing your self-respect. Using the FAST skill is easier when you know yourself and what is important to you. This worksheet will help you build on your understanding of yourself. Remember to use a Non-Judgmental Stance when completing this worksheet so you can notice and appreciate who you are without self-judgment.

What *personal qualities* do you have or want to have? (e.g., "I'm honest," or "I want to be someone who is outgoing.")

_____

_____

_____

_____

_____

What are your *dreams* or *life goals*?

_____

_____

_____

_____

_____

What do you want to do for a *career*? Why?

_____

_____

_____

_____

_____

What are your *top five values* (starting with the most important)?

1. _____   3. _____   5. _____

2. _____   4. _____

Boundaries

Boundaries are limits. Setting boundaries is the way we communicate what is Ok and not Ok in relationships.

You can assert your boundaries in several different areas:

Time: You only have so much time in a day, and it's important to be mindful about how you spend your time. You can assert a boundary with your time by saying no to things you do not want or need to do, or you can say yes to things you want to spend more time on.

Communication: You have the right to be spoken to with respect. People in our lives may say or do hurtful things (at times unintentionally). You can assert a boundary with communication by asking others not to use disrespectful language and to speak to you respectfully.

Personal Items: This includes money, your cell phone, clothes and any property. You can assert a boundary with your personal items by saying no when you are uncomfortable with giving or lending, or you can say yes when you are comfortable with giving or lending.

Physical Space: *Personal space* means the space around you and includes physical touch. You can assert a boundary with your physical space by asking people not to get too close or by saying yes or no to hugs or other forms of physical contact.

Physical Intimacy and Sex: It is important that you determine your own values when it comes to physical intimacy and sex. You can assert a boundary in romantic relationships based on your values. For example, it might be important to you to wait until marriage to have sex, or you might be comfortable with sex outside of marriage. Remember that you have the right to say yes or no to what you are comfortable with.

Personal Information: You have the right not to share things about yourself. You can assert a boundary with personal information by answering or not answering questions that make you uncomfortable and by being mindful about what personal information you share.

Social Media: You have the right to use or not use social media. If you choose to use social media, you can assert a boundary with how others communicate to you on the Internet and with what you post or what others post about you on social media.

Other: _____

_____

Boundaries Evaluation

This worksheet will help you know and assert your Boundaries.

Time Boundaries

What do you want or are willing to spend your time on?

_____

What things do you not want or need to spend your time on?

_____

Communication Boundaries

How do you want people to communicate with you?

_____

What communication are you Ok with from others?

_____

What communication are you not Ok with from others?

_____

Personal Items

To whom are you Ok with giving or lending things?

_____

To whom are you not Ok with giving or lending things?

_____

What things are you Ok with giving or lending?

_____

What things are you not Ok with giving or lending?

_____

Physical Space

How much physical space do you want between yourself and others?

_____

Who are you Ok with touching you?

_____

Who are you not Ok with touching you?

_____

What kind of physical touch are you Ok with?

_____

What kind of physical touch are you not Ok with?

_____

Physical Intimacy and Sex

What are your values when it comes to physical intimacy and sex?

_____

What are you Ok with physically or sexually?

_____

What are you not Ok with physically or sexually?

_____

Personal Information

With whom are you Ok sharing information?

_____

With whom are you not Ok sharing information?

_____

What are you Ok with sharing about yourself?

_____

What information are you not Ok with sharing about yourself?

_____

Social Media

What social media are you Ok with? (e.g., Facebook®, Twitter®, SnapChat®)

_____

What are you Ok with posting on social media?

_____

What are you Ok with others posting about you on social media?

_____

Set Your Boundaries

Here are some tips on how to Set Boundaries with others.

Know what your boundaries are. Remember that your Boundaries might look different than other peoples'. Your Boundaries are not wrong, and it is up to you to figure out what they are.

Review your "Boundaries Evaluation" to remind yourself of your Boundaries. Remember to adjust your Boundaries if you notice they have changed.

Use Interpersonal Effectiveness skills. Use DEAR MAN to assert your Boundaries. Remember to clearly and directly ask for what you want. Be specific if needed.

Use FAST by not apologizing for your Boundaries, and remember to stick to your values!

Use GIVE to be respectful to the other person. Do not blame or judge others for not knowing what your Boundaries are.

Stick to it!! If you set a Boundary of not lending out money and then you give in to a request for money, the other person will be confused about your Boundary and will be more likely to keep asking.

Remember:

- You have a right to say no!

- Meeting your needs will help you be an effective and healthy friend.

- Boundaries are a two-way street. Be mindful of others' boundaries as well.

- Setting boundaries is hard—give yourself credit for trying!

Now that you have learned all the skills in this module, go back to the worksheet "My Relationships Evaluation" on page 75 and fill in the last column with ways that you can use the Interpersonal Effectiveness skills in each of your relationships.

Interpersonal Effectiveness Skills List

The Interpersonal Effectiveness module teaches skills to improve relationships.

A2R	Attend to Relationships	Care for your relationships
G	GIVE	Build healthy relationships
DM	DEAR MAN	Assert yourself, ask for what you want, say no
F	FAST	Focus on your self-respect in relationships

Part Two

DBT for Parents

DBT Can Help You, Too!

While your teenager is going through a difficult time, you are likely going through a difficult time as well. The good news is that DBT can help you, too. DBT offers you, as parents, skills to cope and act effectively with this difficult time. The parent section of this book addresses underlying themes and concepts common to the parents of teenagers with mental health concerns. The goal is to help parents enhance their understanding of the dynamics that may be playing out in their household. Parents will learn to apply these concepts to their own teen-parent relationship.

Parents will begin by learning about adolescent-specific Dialectical Dilemmas, as first identified by Miller, Rathus and Linehan (2007) in their book, *Dialectical Behavior Therapy with Suicidal Adolescents*. Learning to find balance with Dialectical Dilemmas will help parents:

- Encourage healthy development through adolescence.

- Effectively respond to crisis behaviors.

- Find balance between being too strict and too lenient.

- Learn ways to offer your teen support *and* encourage independence.

- Avoid blaming yourself or others for your teen's mental health concerns so you can focus on influencing (but not forcing) growth and change.

Parents will then learn skills to parent from Wise Mind. This means having a balanced approach by making decisions based both emotions and the facts. Parents will learn to:

- Recognize your State of Mind.

- Validate and accept difficult emotions.

- Manage difficult emotions so they do not get in the way of effective parenting.

Parents will learn to bring Wise Mind to life through Mindfulness skills. Parents will learn Mindfulness skills to:

- Parent with mindfulness of your own thoughts and emotions.

- Focus on one step at a time.

- Avoid judging yourself and your teen.

- Act Effectively to meet your goals.

Parents will learn relationship skills to improve the connection and communication with their teen. This includes:

- Using the GIVE skill to build up the relationship with your teen.

- Increase assertiveness with the DEAR MAN skill.

- Recognize and live consistently with your values as a parent.

Parents will learn to improve Self-Care to help manage the difficult emotions and situations that arise when parenting a teenager. Parents will learn to:

- Improve physical health with the PLEASE skill.

- Recognize strengths and weaknesses with Self-Care.

- Create family goals for improved health.

Last, parents will learn the CARES skill to improve consistency in setting rules, expectations and consequences and create predictability at home.

Dialectical Dilemmas

A Dialectical Dilemma occurs when one feels stuck between two ideas that seem opposite to each other (Linehan, 1993a). The focus in DBT is to find *balance* by incorporating elements from both sides of the dialectic. In other words, the goal is to avoid being on one end of the extreme or the other and instead find balance in the middle.

Three adolescent-specific Dialectical Dilemmas were identified by Miller, Rathus and Linehan (2007) in their book *Dialectical Behavior Therapy with Suicidal Adolescents*. These Dialectical Dilemmas are common and important for parents to know and understand, as parents are most effective when they incorporate elements from both sides of the spectrum in these dialectics.

Allowing Developmentally Typical Behaviors vs. Addressing Problem Behaviors. Finding balance with this dialectic means letting teenagers practice their developmental tasks while taking seriously behaviors that are beyond what one would expect developmentally. This requires parents to differentiate between developmentally typical and more serious problem behaviors.

Being Strict vs. Being Lenient. Finding balance with this dialectic means having expectations, rules or limits while also being flexible. This requires parents to identify rules and consequences, while also using their Wise Mind to determine when some slack is needed.

Fostering Independence vs. Giving Support. Finding balance with this dialectic means supporting a teen's primary developmental task of gaining autonomy by providing space for him or her to make decisions while also providing structure, support and problem solving. This requires parents to recognize and act effectively with their own thoughts and emotions about their teen being independent.

Included here is a new Dialectical Dilemma, which addresses a common thinking pattern that acts as a barrier to parents engaging effectively with their teenagers.

Blame Self vs. Blame Others. Finding balance with this dialectic means not blaming yourself or others for your teen's mental health concerns. Assigning blame creates difficult emotions and actually gets in the way of change. Balance is found with Radical Acceptance, which helps parents to accept that they cannot change or control their teenager. This frees parents up to focus on ways to influence (but not control) a teen's decisions and behavior.

Parents are encouraged to complete worksheets associated with each Dialectical Dilemma so that they can best bring to life balance.

What Is Typical, What Is Not?

Remember that development is different for each individual. For some teens, developmentally typical behaviors can be taken to an extreme and become a greater problem. Parents have a difficult task here, as they need to both allow for developmentally typical behaviors *and* address problem behaviors (Miller, Rathus & Linehan, 2007).

DEVELOPMENTALLY TYPICAL BEHAVIORS	BALANCE	PROBLEM BEHAVIORS

Allow Developmentally Typical Behaviors. Developmentally typical behaviors include challenging behaviors that are the result of the developmental tasks of adolescence . In other words, these are behaviors that are common and expected for adolescents but are also difficult to encounter and interact with.

Examples include frequent arguments with parents, minor violations of the rules (such as missing curfew) and refusal to talk about emotions or school tasks.

See the next sections for a detailed discussion of the developmental tasks of adolescence.

It is helpful for parents to know and recognize what is developmentally expected (Miller, Rathus & Linehan, 2007). It is important that parents not overreact to these developmentally typical behaviors. It is the parent's job to weather these storms and support his or her teen in the growing pains of development. Sometimes this support means having flexibility so that the teen can work through his or her developmental tasks.

Address Problem Behaviors. Problem behaviors stem from developmentally typical behaviors but have reached an extreme. These are difficult behaviors that are more concerning or serious than the challenging behaviors typically seen in adolescence (Miller, Rathus & Linehan, 2007). Problem behaviors can create large consequences, are often harmful and reduce the quality of life for the teen and his or her family.

Problem behaviors are an extreme form of developmentally expected behaviors. Examples include self-injury, suicide attempts, mental health hospitalization and addiction issues.

It is helpful for parents to know and recognize what behaviors are beyond typical. It is important for parents to take these behaviors seriously, as they require less flexibility than the developmentally typical behaviors.

Remember to think about difficult adolescent behaviors as dialectic, and note that problem behaviors occur on the other end of the spectrum from developmentally typical adolescent behaviors. Consider the following example:

> Brianna gets in a fight with her mom about doing chores and as a result of the fight, yells, "I hate you," runs up to her room, slams her door and gives her mom the silent treatment for the rest of the day. The next day, Brianna's behavior is back to normal.

Although these behaviors are not pleasant and are difficult to experience and accept, they do not cause long-term harm for Brianna and her family. These behaviors are developmentally typical for adolescents.

Now consider an example on the other end of the dialectic:

> Brianna gets in a fight with her mom about doing chores, yells "I hate you," runs up to her room, slams her door and injures herself by cutting her arm. She doesn't talk to her mom for the rest of the day but the following day discloses her self-injury to a school counselor, who later informs Brianna's mom. When her mom asks about it, Brianna says, "It's none of your business" and refuses to talk to her about it.

Some of Brianna's behaviors are developmentally expected for adolescents. Arguing, slamming her door and refusing to talk to her mom about her emotions and behaviors are developmentally typical. However, using self-injury to cope with an argument is more extreme and is a problem behavior. This behavior will have bigger consequences for her and her family.

Balance. There are many factors that can make it difficult to find balance in this dialectic. When teens have mental health concerns, it can be easy to become desensitized to crisis behaviors, and parents can get into the habit of treating problem behaviors with more flexibility than needed (Miller, Rathus & Linehan, 2007). Conversely, parents can also begin to see every difficult behavior as a problem behavior and end up not using as much flexibility as they could with developmentally typical behaviors (Miller, Rathus & Linehan, 2007).

Balance in this area means giving support and flexibility to your teenager's developmentally typical behaviors while taking seriously and addressing problem behaviors. In the second example, Brianna's mom's main focus should be on Brianna's self-injury and problem solving ways to help her daughter maintain safety. The following sections will provide you with information to help you find balance in allowing developmentally typical behaviors and addressing problem behaviors.

Adolescence: Developmental Tasks

Developmental tasks are new skills or abilities that we learn and achieve during particular stages of life. Developmental tasks help us to move forward in our physical, mental and emotional growth. Learning these new tasks is what helps us grow up to become effective and well-adjusted adults. Acquiring new abilities and skills in each stage of development can be difficult, and people going through stages of development tend to not be very good at each new task at first. This can create frustration for both the child and the parents.

Knowing and reminding yourself of the developmental tasks of adolescence can help you recognize what is typical—what to expect during the teenage years. Keep in mind that development is unique for each individual. Some of the tasks listed here may or may not occur with your teenager.

Establishing an Identity. Teenagers are trying to figure out who they are. This involves integrating the opinions of others, such as parents and friends, into their own understanding of themselves (McNeely & Blachard, 2010). The goal of this developmental task is to have a clear sense of their own opinions, values and beliefs and to figure out how they fit into their world.

What you might see in your teen:

- Spending a lot of time in his or her room alone.
- Not wanting to spend time with family.
- Experimentation with different types of music, clothes, makeup, jobs, interests, friend groups.
- Trying out hobbies or clubs.
- Experimentation with alcohol and drugs or sex.
- Daydreaming.
- Spending more time with friends than family.

Establishing Independence and Autonomy. Teenagers are working on independence and finding their own way in the world. This means making their own decisions and living by their own sense of what is right and wrong (McNeely & Blachard, 2010). Teenagers are focused on being less dependent on their parents, and often push their parents and family away. This pushing away is about making room for their own decisions and acting independently.

What you might see in your teen:

- Not talking to parents about school, relationships or emotions.
- Not wanting to be seen with parents or family in public.
- Spending more time with friends than family.
- Being more argumentative or critical with parents.
- Being reluctant to share where he or she is going or with whom he or she is spending time.
- Rejecting parent's help or support.
- Having mood swings.
- Being disinterested in or rejecting of things he or she enjoyed in childhood.
- Breaking rules or boundaries set by parents.

Practicing Intimacy and Closeness in Relationships. Teenagers are focused on and interested in peer relationships and are finding new ways to be more intimate with others (McNeely & Blachard, 2010). This can include emotional and sexual intimacy. Often this intimacy occurs with same-sex friendships but can also include a significant other.

What you might see in your teen:

- Intense friendships.
- Strong peer alliances and acting in ways similar to peers.
- A strong connection with a group of friends.
- A lot of time spent talking, texting or hanging out with friends or peers.
- A lot of time spent focused on a "crush" or love interest.
- Curiosity about sex and intimacy.
- Exploration of physical intimacy such as dating and sex.

Adjusting to a Developing and Changing Body. Teenagers experience significant changes in their bodies. Teens often become over-focused on their appearance (McNeely & Blanchard, 2012) and the appearance of others. This can cause them to be self-conscious or have difficulty figuring out how to dress or how they want to appear to others.

What you might see in your teen:

- Taking a long time to get dressed.
- Preoccupation with appearance.
- Increased interest in looking attractive.
- Focus on how others look.
- Acting shy or self-conscious.

Adjusting to Brain Development. Teenagers also experience significant changes in brain development. Teens are becoming better at reasoning and can now consider many options and think about things hypothetically (McNeely & Blanchard, 2010). Teenagers are acquiring the new skill of thinking abstractly, meaning they can think about what cannot be seen, heard or touched. This means they may be considering their own beliefs and values, which involve abstract ideas like trust and loyalty. Although teens have new cognitive skills, the area of the brain responsible for planning and identifying long-term consequences is not yet fully developed, so although they can see the abstract, they are still not very skilled with planning and thinking ahead.

What you might see in your teen:

- Belief that he or she can take risks without severe consequences.
- Focus on life's greater meaning.
- Thoughts about how others see him or her.
- Greater focus on what he or she thinks and how he or she feels.
- Belief that everyone else is as concerned with his or her thoughts and behaviors as he or she is.
- Belief that he or she is the only one who has these thoughts and feelings.

- Being dramatic due to a belief that no one else has felt how he or she feels.
- Difficulty seeing the shades of gray.
- Questioning family's religious or spiritual beliefs.

The developmental tasks of adolescence can be particularly frustrating and confusing to parents as well as to teens. It is helpful to understand how the actions of your teenager are developmentally typical. Additionally, parents can be effective during such a difficult period of development by finding ways to support their teen's developmental tasks.

Problem Behaviors

On the opposite end of the dialectic from developmentally typical behaviors are problem behaviors. Remember that problem behaviors are an extreme form of developmentally expected behaviors (Miller, Rathus & Linehan, 2007). Problem behaviors can vary greatly depending on the individual.

As mentioned earlier, a behavior may be a problem when (Miller, Rathus & Linehan, 2007):

- The behavior creates more severe consequences (especially in the long term).
- The behavior creates physical or emotional harm.
- The behavior significantly reduces the quality of life for the teen and his or her family.

Problem behaviors can include:

- Suicidal thoughts or suicide attempts
- Self-injury (such as cutting, burning the skin)
- Using drugs and alcohol (beyond experimentation) or addiction
- Over-eating, restricting or purging
- Promiscuity
- Refusal to go to school and truancy
- Complete disengagement from parents
- Running away from home

Problem behaviors can be maladaptive attempts to cope with a crisis. Many people have difficulty finding effective ways to deal with intense situations. Problem behaviors can be developed as a way to get through a difficult situation. These maladaptive attempts to cope, or problem behaviors, then continue because they provided relief, so people will continue to turn to that behavior when other difficult situations arise.

Although problem behaviors serve a purpose, they also come with big downsides. These downsides can include:

- Physical harm
- Hospitalization
- Conflict with others
- Loss of relationships
- Lack of self-care

- Decreased self-respect
- Failing grades
- Suspension or expulsion from school
- Health issues

Problem behaviors that create risks to someone's safety are especially important to understand and take action on.

Suicidal Ideation (SI). This includes any thoughts of suicide, from passive thoughts to more active, planful thoughts. For example, passive thoughts might include, "My family would be better off without me," and more active thoughts could include plans of how to commit suicide, which can lead to gathering the means to commit suicide and taking action on a suicide plan.

Self-Injurious Behavior (SIB). This includes any urges to or behaviors that harm oneself, without the intent to end one's life. Examples of SIB include cutting, scratching or burning the skin.

Teenagers who struggle with SI or SIB require professional help, and it is important that these teenagers are receiving mental health treatment. Therapy will help teens identify triggers for SI or SIB and create safety plans to manage thoughts and urges for suicide or self-injury. Mental health professionals are trained in how to assess safety and help create plans and interventions to ensure a teenagers' safety.

Safety issues are understandably scary for parents. Parents should take safety concerns seriously. This is a time to be focused on problem solving to ensure that teenagers are safe. It is important for parents to take a Non-Judgmental Stance toward safety issues and avoid statements that may be shaming. Remember that safety issues are a maladaptive attempt to cope with stress. Ask your teen to share his or her safety plan and how you can help with safety. If your teen is suicidal and unable to stay safe, take him or her to the nearest emergency room for a safety assessment from a mental health professional.

Parents need to make decisions about how to intervene with their teen's behaviors. Parents should strive for balance by allowing for developmentally appropriate behaviors while taking seriously and addressing problem behaviors. The challenge in finding this balance often requires parents to learn and practice new skills. The following worksheets provide the opportunity to work on these skills.

Typical vs. Problem Behaviors - Balance in Action

Identifying developmentally typical and problem behaviors takes knowledge, patience and practice. Take some time to reflect on difficult situations with your teen.

Describe a difficult situation you encountered with your teen. Include details and focus on the facts:

_____

_____

_____

_____

_____

Write down the developmentally typical behaviors you noticed from your teen during this situation:

_____

_____

_____

_____

_____

Write out problem behaviors (or behaviors more extreme than the developmentally typical behaviors) you noticed from your teen during this situation that are more extreme than developmentally typical behaviors:

_____

_____

_____

_____

Try this reflection several times to increase your non-judgmental awareness of your teen's behaviors.

_____

_____

_____

Being Strict vs. Lenient

The second Dialectical Dilemma is between being Strict and being Lenient. Remember that the parent's goal with our Dialectical Dilemmas is to find balance between these two extremes.

STRICT	BALANCE	LENIENT

Being Strict

Parents on this end of the dialectic are often referred to as authoritarian. Parents who are too strict have many rules and expectations and weighty consequences for not following the rules (Miller, Rathus & Linehan, 2007). Parents on this end of the extreme often do not give options and have high expectations for performance or achievement. These parents may not give much emotional support or warmth and are focused on discipline.

There are some effective elements from this end of the dialectic. Being strict gives teenagers limitations and specific expectations. This can help teens avoid getting into trouble and promote success in school or other activities. However, this end of the dialectic also comes with some significant consequences. Being too strict or rigid prevents teens from successfully building independence. High expectations and weighty consequences can lead to perfectionism and a sense that the teen is always in trouble or is not good enough. Parenting at this end of the spectrum can prevent emotional growth and leads to disconnected or strained teen-parent relationships.

Being Lenient

Parents on this end of the dialectic are often referred to as permissive or uninvolved. Parents who are too lenient give their teens a lot of freedom and have few rules or expectations for their behavior (Miller, Rathus & Linehan, 2007). The rules that do exist may be inconsistent or not enforced. Parents on this end of the dialectic can either be too emotionally involved or warm or may lack warmth or emotional involvement. Parents who are overly warm are often described as being their teen's "friend" rather than parent. Parents who are not emotionally involved may expect their teenager to fend for himself or herself.

This side of the dialectic also has effective elements. Teens have lots of room to explore and build independence, which can lead to creativity and new skills. The downside is that teens don't have limitations or guidance, which can lead to problem behaviors. Teens with parents who are too lenient can have unreasonable expectations about how much freedom and leniency they should receive in other settings, such as school, work or relationships. Additionally, teens may feel unimportant, and the lack of expectations can lead them to feel not cared about.

Balance

Parents who find balance with this dialectic are often referred to as authoritative. These parents have expectations, rules or limits for their teens *and* have flexibility and leniency (Miller, Rathus & Linehan, 2007). In other words, parents who find this balance are mindful about the battles they pick, have clear and fair consequences and allow their teens room to make mistakes and some freedom to make their own choices. Parents on this end of the dialectic encourage discussion with their teen about his or her opinions and choices.

There are many positive impacts of this style of parenting. Teens will have both freedom to build independence and guidance to help them avoid significant mistakes. Teens will also be likely to feel valued and important and will have healthy emotional connections with their parents, allowing them to reach out to them to discuss difficult topics. These teens will be more likely to have confidence in their abilities.

Dialectical Challenges

Finding balance on this dialectic can be difficult when parenting a teen with mental health concerns. Difficult emotions such as fear, frustration or guilt can lead parents to be too strict in an attempt to control and avoid their teen's problem behaviors (Miller, Rathus & Linehan, 2007). Often the result of this is an increase in the teen's depression, anxiety or anger, worsening of the situation and persistence of problem behaviors.

Difficult emotions can also lead parents to be too lenient in an attempt to avoid triggering their teen and his or her problem behaviors (Miller, Rathus & Linehan, 2007). This, too, can lead to a worsening of the situation and persistence of problem behaviors.

At times, a parent will swing from one of the dialectic to the other. A parent may begin by being too lenient, allowing an excess of freedom. Then, when trouble arises, the parent swings to the other end of the dialectic by being too strict, creating too many rules and expectations and employing excessive consequences (Miller, Rathus & Linehan, 2007). When being too strict creates conflict or an increase in mental health concerns, the parent may again swing to the other extreme and become too lenient. Vacillating between extremes sends mixed messages to the teen and requires the parent to use skillful means to strike balance between the two.

There are many factors that make finding balance with this dialectic difficult. The following worksheets will help you consider ways to create balance.

Being Strict vs. Lenient - Balance in Action

Following are some suggestions to help you find balance between being Strict and being Lenient.

Relationship First

Building an effective and connected relationship with your teen is an important and primary factor in finding balance between being too strict and too lenient. Having a solid relationship with your teen will make setting limits and offering support easier, as it promotes mutual respect and increases the chance that your teen will talk to and work with you. Keep in mind that putting the relationship first does not mean trying to be your teen's friend. You are still the parent. Putting the relationship first means being genuine, placing importance on your connection and working to improve the relationship.

There are many ways to build a relationship with your teenager. Here are some suggestions:

- Invite your teenager to engage in mutual interests or hobbies. If you both like watching football or going shopping, offer an invitation to do these things together. Your teen may or may not take you up on the offer, but sometimes even an invitation can make a difference.

- Be mindful of shared experiences, such as making a meal together, watching a TV show or time in the car together. Be present in moments that you have with your teen. Avoid distractions during these experiences, and use them as a chance for positive interaction.

- Laugh and have fun! There is a lot to be serious about, but it is also important for your teen to see your lighter side.

- Look for opportunities for discussion. Think about questions you can ask your teen about life and values. Find out what he or she thinks, how he or she would respond in certain situations and reasons for his or her opinions. Talk about controversial subjects, but avoid lecturing. Remember, your goal is to hear your teen's opinions. Consider only sharing your opinions if your teen asks.

- When your teen has positive news, talk about it and ask questions to understand what happened and how it made him or her feel. Have conversations about what went well, and share your positive experiences and accomplishments with your teen.

- _____

  _____

- _____

  _____

The GIVE skill is an excellent way to build your relationship with your teenager. See the section titled "GIVE: Put Relationship First," on page 150, to bring this to life.

Focus on the Positive

In parenting teens with mental health issues, it can be easy to over-focus on what is not going well. However, over-focusing on problem behaviors and having too many rules or expectations creates a negative environment that can leave your teenager feeling discouraged. In the long term, this over- focus on the negative causes your teenager to associate you with difficult feelings and being in trouble. This can strain your relationship and get in the way of creating a supportive parent-child bond. Giving too much attention to ineffective behaviors can also actually reinforce those ineffective behaviors.

It is important to recognize what is working and areas in which your teenager is doing well (Miller, Rathus & Linehan, 2007). Keep in mind that this does not mean ignoring what isn't going well. Rather, the idea is to find balance by bringing in a greater focus on successes, no matter how small. This can boost your teen's confidence, improve your relationship and teaches the Give Myself Credit skill (see page 63).

An important first step in focusing on the positive is learning to be mindful of small improvements. It is uncommon for people to make big changes quickly. Instead, change is often made up of very small steps. If you are not looking for them, these small steps can be easy to miss.

So, what do you look for in focusing on the positive? Start by identifying target behaviors. Target behaviors are actions that you would like to see more of from your teen. The idea behind target behaviors is having specific behaviors or areas to which you will pay attention that will help you notice small changes. Target behaviors can be goals that you and your teen discuss and set or areas you think are important to pay attention to. The goal of setting target behaviors is to increase mindfulness of the positives and progress with specific behaviors.

Remember to keep your target behaviors reasonable. For example, you may feel it is important for your teen to have a clean room, but perhaps this goal is too big for your teen to accomplish right away. Your teen may make small steps toward this goal by putting dirty clothes in the hamper or making the bed. Although his or her room is not clean, there has been progress in that area. These small steps are important to notice and can become target behaviors.

Start by identifying two to four target behaviors on which to focus:

1. _____

_____

2. _____

_____

3. _____

_____

4. _____

_____

Your goal is to pay attention to these behaviors or even small approximations of the behaviors (e.g., putting some clean clothes away) and reinforce them when they happen.

Having target behaviors does not mean that you ignore other effective decisions or behaviors; instead, having target behaviors will help you notice some of the effective things your teen is doing.

Positive reinforcement is the next step. The idea is that people are more likely to do things for which they are reinforced.

You can reinforce target behaviors in many ways. Consider what your teen may respond to and add additional ideas:

- Say something simple, like "Way to go" or "I noticed how great you did there."

- Give him or her credit: "That was such a great idea."

- Tell your teen, "I'm proud of you for accomplishing that."

- Make a special meal or stop to get a treat.

- Offer a reward—even a small one like extra TV time.

- _____

- _____

When using reinforcement, make sure it is clear that the reinforcement is for the positive change. Also try to be consistent in offering reinforcement and remember not to damper this positive focus with negative statements or refocusing on what is not going well. Instead, let the reinforcement stand on its own, and find another time to discuss trouble areas. Try to reinforce as soon as you notice the change or that the target behavior has been met.

Your teen may have a negative reaction to your reinforcement. Sometimes this is because he or she is embarrassed or has low self-confidence. Remember not to over-do your reinforcement, and be genuine in how you are expressing it. Despite a negative reaction, continue to offer reinforcement in small but meaningful ways.

Set Limits

The other end of the dialectic is focusing on areas that require rules or limits. Teens need boundaries and guidance. Parents need to be active in identifying and setting rules.

Just as identifying target behaviors helps you to narrow your focus, it is advisable to identify a few areas for which you wish to set limits or make rules. Choosing your battles becomes easier when you have thought about and set rules in some important areas. This also allows you to be mindful of ways you wish to be flexible. The goal is not to have rules and limits over everything, but rather to have rules and expectations for the most important areas.

Consider working together with your teen to set rules and limits. Try having a discussion with him or her, and be careful not to lecture. Ask your teen about the pros and cons of a rule or limit and in what areas he or she needs to be accountable. Involving your teen can increase investment in the rules and limits, and make it more likely that he or she will comply. Having your teen involved in setting rules is a nice way to enhance your relationship. It also promotes independence, teaches self-discipline and helps him or her see rules less as things imposed by you and more as standards he or she wishes to live up to. Listen to and try to incorporate your teen's ideas but remember that you are the parent and have the final say in rules and limits. Consider giving an explanation if you set a rule that is different from what your teen requests.

Consider including all parents and step-parents in discussions about the rules and limits. Remember that if needed, setting rules and limits can occur over the course of several conversations. If there is conflict or difficult emotions arise from working with each other, taking a break and returning to the conversation later can be an effective strategy.

List your initial thoughts about rules and limits. Remember to focus on the most important areas first:

1. _____

_____

2. _____

_____

3. _____

_____

4. _____

_____

Once the rules and limits have been determined, set clear consequences if they are broken. Again, consider involving your teen and other parents or step-parents in a discussion about consequences. Make sure they are appropriate for the rule and are not big or too small. Ruling with an iron fist tends to produce unwanted results, as teens can demonstrate more rule-breaking or limit testing.

List some possible consequences here:

1. _____

_____

2. _____

_____

3. _____

_____

4. _____

_____

When the rules, limits and consequences have been solidified, make sure to communicate them to the household. Consider putting them in writing, and make the document accessible to all involved. Being on the same page with your teenager and other parents will help to increase consistency and make enforcing the rules more straightforward.

Remember to be consistent in enforcing the rules, limits and boundaries. In other words, follow through with your plan. Doing so will help your teens know what to expect and will teach accountability. See the section titled: *CARES: A Skill for Consistency* on page 163 to learn more about ways to be consistent.

Independence vs. Support

The next Dialectical Dilemma is between encouraging independence and offering support. Remember that the parent's goal with Dialectical Dilemmas is to find balance between these extremes.

INDEPENDENCE   BALANCE   SUPPORT

Encouraging Independence

On this end of the dialectic, parents encourage independence and autonomy. This is a developmental task of adolescence that helps teens gain skills and responsibility, as well as create a sense of self separate from family.

Taken to an extreme, encouraging independence can be a problem. Parents who encourage too much autonomy may have adult expectations for their teen and hold him or her to a standard he or she has not yet reached developmentally (Miller, Rathus & Linehan, 2007). This could include expectations of emotional maturity, maintaining the household, caring for younger siblings or paying bills. Although teens need to learn responsibility to be successful as adults, they are not yet adults and still require support and guidance. Parents on this end of the dialectic stifle the development of independence, as their teenager is required to take on too much too quickly.

Offering Support

On this end of the dialectic, parents offer support, guidance and problem solving, which teens need.

Taken to an extreme, parents become excessive caretakers and take on too much responsibility for elements of their teenager's life (Miller, Rathus & Linehan, 2007). There may not be clear boundaries between the teen and parent. Parents on this end of the dialectic may solve problems for their teen, rather than support the teen in solving problems himself or herself. Parents on this end of the dialectic also stifle their adolescent's natural development of independence, as he or she is not given the space to make decisions or mistakes or take ownership over his or her own problems or daily tasks.

Balance

Balance with this dialectic involves encouraging teenagers to take responsibility for some elements of their life *and* giving support and problem solving in other areas. By finding balance here, parents are best supporting the developmental task of autonomy.

Each teenager is different, and areas for support or independence will vary. Completing homework, scheduling extracurricular activities and addressing problems with teachers are examples of areas where a teenager could take responsibility. When teens are "in charge" of areas of their life, they are learning independence and have the freedom they need to manage daily tasks in their own way (Miller, Rathus & Linehan, 2007). Balance can be found here with the parent offering suggestions or support if the management of these daily stressors becomes too difficult or the teen asks for help.

Support vs. Independence - Balance in Action

It can be a difficult to balance independence and support with your teenager. This evaluation will help you figure out what you need to work toward this balance. Teenagers also complete this evaluation in the Interpersonal Effectiveness section of this book. Spend some time considering areas for which teens could be responsible and areas in which you would like to have more influence. When each of you have competed this worksheet, spend some time comparing notes.

Independence—What things do you think your teenager could handle independently?

Home (examples: choosing his or her own bedtime, completing chores without reminders)
School (examples: keeping track of assignments and grades, asking the teacher for help)
Friends/Peers (examples: arranging plans with friends, setting limits with peers)
Other Areas:

Support—In what areas do you feel your teen still needs support and guidance?

Home (examples: check on teen when self-injury urges are high, give reminders to take medication)

School (examples: reminders of due dates, homework help):

Friends/Peers (examples: meeting your teen's friends, knowing where he or she is going)

Other Areas:

Acceptance is Key

Parents can have thought and belief patterns that get in the way of acting effectively with their teen. One difficult thought pattern can be blaming yourself or blaming others for your teen's mental health concerns. Let's look at this dialectic:

BLAME SELF   RADICAL ACCEPTANCE   BLAME OTHERS

Blame Self

Another term for blaming yourself is *personalization*. When parents blame themselves, they are taking responsibility for their teen's mental health or decisions. Blaming yourself can also mean seeing what your teen does as a direct reflection on you.

Some examples include thinking you are a bad parent because your teen has anxiety or thinking you did something wrong because your teen got a D in a class.

The problem with this thought pattern is that parents do not have control over their teen's mental health or decisions. Parents who find themselves on this end of the dialectic may end up pressuring their kids, often because their confidence as a parent has become dependent on how well their teen is doing. Alternatively, parents may end up doing too much for their teen in an effort to "fix" the situation. These beliefs and behaviors can actually get in the way of their teen getting better.

Blame Others

Parents can also end up blaming others for their teen's mental health issues. This could include blaming your spouse, teachers, therapists or the teen.

Some examples include blaming your spouse for your teen's bad grades because your spouse let your teen go out with friends during the week or blaming your teen for self-injury because he or she is "not working hard enough."

The problem with this thought pattern is that this blame is often unfounded and creates guilt and shame. This makes a difficult situation even worse. Parents who find themselves on this end of the dialectic may be over-focused on big changes and will not recognize small improvements. These parents may not see how they are contributing to difficult situations. This, too, can get in the way of teens getting better.

Radical Acceptance

Finding the middle ground means practicing Radical Acceptance. With Radical Acceptance, you do not blame yourself or others. Instead, notice and accept your strengths and weaknesses in helping your teen with his or her mental health concerns and also notice and accept other's strengths and weaknesses. With acceptance, you are being non-judgmental and are working with the facts (Linehan, 1993b). Remember that Radical Acceptance does not mean giving up or pretending things are good the way they are. Instead, Radical Acceptance means simply knowing and acknowledging what is. In other words, with acceptance, you are no longer fighting what you cannot change. Acceptance means working from where you are—not where you want to be or the way you think things "should" be.

For parents, acceptance means recognizing that your teen's choices are not your choices, and that his or her struggles are not your responsibility to fix. It is your role to support and help your teen, but ultimately your teen's choices are his or her own. Blaming yourself or others for everything does not help and can create suffering.

Turn the Mind - Move Forward with Acceptance

Using Radical Acceptance can be tough. This worksheet will help you practice Radical Acceptance with your teenager. The goal is to identify what thoughts get in the way of acceptance. The skill Turn the Mind will then help you turn your thoughts toward acceptance (Linehan, 1993b).

Our thoughts have a big impact on how we feel and act. Take a look at the following example:

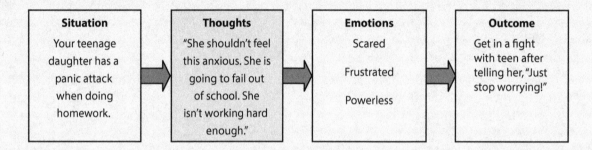

Situation	**Thoughts**	**Emotions**	**Outcome**
Your teenage daughter has a panic attack when doing homework.	"She shouldn't feel this anxious. She is going to fail out of school. She isn't working hard enough."	Scared Frustrated Powerless	Get in a fight with teen after telling her, "Just stop worrying!"

We cannot change many of the situations we experience. As a parent you will not be able to change many situations you encounter with your teenager. Notice in the above example how the parent's thoughts are focused on the daughter feeling or doing something different. Although it makes sense for the parent to want this, these thoughts are focused on what the parent wants rather than what is. This makes it difficult for the parent to empathize and effectively problem solve.

Here are examples of thoughts that parents often experience that are non-accepting. Check those that may apply to you and add others that you notice:

☐ "I never went through that when I was his/her age."

☐ "He/she shouldn't feel this way."

☐ "He/she isn't working hard enough."

☐ "This is just a phase."

☐ "I must have done something wrong as a parent."

☐ "This will never get better."

☐ "He/she shouldn't be acting this way."

☐ "He/she's just lazy."

☐ _____

☐ _____

☐ _____

Remember not to judge these thoughts. They are common and are an attempt to cope with a difficult situation. Although we can understand where these thoughts come from, we must also recognize that these thoughts take you further from acceptance and often make the situation more difficult. This is where Turn the Mind comes in. The goal of Turn the Mind is to look at the same situation (which you often cannot control) with acceptance.

Let's look at how to use Turn the Mind in the same situation. Remember that the goal is to focus on thoughts that lead to acceptance.

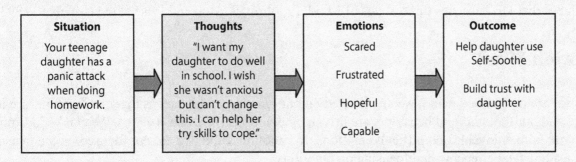

In this example, notice how the parent's thoughts still include a desire for things to be different. This time, however, the parent is also recognizing that she cannot force her daughter's anxiety to change. This allowed the parent to focus on how she could influence the situation by helping her daughter with skills. Notice also that the parent's emotions do not change drastically. However, by focusing her thoughts on acceptance, she feels more capable in a difficult situation.

Here are examples of thoughts lead to acceptance with your teenager. Check those that may apply to you, and add others that you notice:

☐ "I cannot control my son/daughter's emotions and choices."

☐ "My role is to support and help."

☐ "I can offer to help her/him use DBT skills."

☐ "I can deal with this."

☐ "I want things to be different, but I can't force things to change."

☐ _____

☐ _____

☐ _____

Parenting From Wise Mind

EMOTION MIND	WISE MIND	REASON MIND

Remember that DBT teaches three States of Mind, Emotion, Reason and Wise Mind (Linehan, 1993b).

Emotion Mind

When we are in Emotion Mind, we are focused on our emotions. This means that our emotions are in charge, and our thoughts and behaviors are driven by emotions (Linehan, 1993b). We can be in Emotion Mind with both enjoyable and difficult emotions. In Emotion Mind, we are *not* focused on the facts and are instead just experiencing and focusing on emotions.

When parents are in Emotion Mind, they are not thinking about what is most effective and are instead making decisions based on how they are feeling in the moment. When parents act from Emotion Mind, their kids may feel that they are not being heard or helped. In difficult situations, acting from Emotion Mind does not help a teenager manage his or her problem behaviors and often causes a parent to unintentionally make the event worse or reinforce the problem behavior.

Some examples of parenting from Emotion Mind include:

- Parent refusing to take his or her teen to the emergency room due to guilt and shame about his/her teen's self-injury.

- Parent yelling at his or her teen when angry.

- Parent looking through his or her teen's emails and texts because of fears of who his or her friends are.

- _____

- _____

Reason Mind

When we are in Reason Mind, we are focused on the facts (Linehan, 1993b). This means that we are analyzing and thinking logically. In Reason Mind, our thoughts and behaviors are guided by facts. We are *not* focused on or feeling much emotion in Reason Mind.

When parents are in Reason Mind, they are analyzing and thinking about logical solutions to their teen's mental health concerns. Parents in Reason Mind are not feeling their own feelings or seeing and empathizing with their teen's emotions. When parents act from Reason Mind, their kids may feel invalidated or misunderstood.

Some examples of parenting from Reason Mind include:

- Parent tells his or her teen, "Just stop worrying."

- When teen shares that he or she had a bad day, parent only offers advice about what to do differently.

- Parent over-focuses on the details of a troubling situation and misses hearing what his or her teen needs.

- _____

- _____

Wise Mind

When we are in Wise Mind, we are able to feel our emotions *and* focus on the facts (Linehan, 1993b). In Wise Mind, we make decisions based both on emotions and the facts. Wise Mind helps us do what is healthy and effective.

When parents are in Wise Mind, they are able to balance their emotions, their teen's emotions and the facts. Parenting from Wise Mind means making decisions based both on emotions and the facts. This allows parents to act effectively in difficult situations. When parents are in Wise Mind, their kids are likely to feel validated *and* helped.

Some examples of parenting from Wise Mind include:

- Parent uses Self-Soothe by deep breathing with teen when he or she is feeling anxious.

- Parent notices feeling scared when learning about self-injury and calls a friend for support.

- Parent notices feeling angry and takes a break from a conflict with his or her teen.

- _____

- _____

This book offers suggestions and ideas to consider in parenting your teenager. However, difficult situations that arise with teens, particularly those associated with Dialectical Dilemmas, do not have one "right" answer or formula to follow. Often there are complicating circumstances, and parenting decisions can vary with each child and in each situation. The relationship with your teenager can be complicated, and intense emotions can be involved in navigating the many struggles that arise. This is why learning to parent from Wise Mind is essential (Miller, Rathus, Linehan, 2007). Parents are most likely to make effective decisions when they are working from their Wise Mind.

Wise Mind has been compared to intuition or a "gut sense" of what is needed in the situation (Linehan, 1993b). Each person has a Wise Mind, and Wise Mind is truly about being centered in yourself and your environment, listening to your intuition. Wise Mind requires non-judgmentally noticing your emotions and the facts and making mindful and planned decisions that promote wellness.

Parenting from Wise Mind requires awareness of your State of Mind in the moment. If you notice being in Emotion or Reason Mind, you can then make adjustments in thinking and acting that will lead you again to Wise Mind.

Worksheet

Identify Your State of Mind

To parent from Wise Mind, it is important to learn how to identify your States of Mind. Think about each State of Mind and jot some notes about what you notice when you are in Emotion, Reason or Wise Mind. What you notice for each State of Mind becomes a "red flag," to which you can then pay attention in the moment. Noticing these red flags will help you make mindful decisions about how to access Wise Mind.

	Emotion Mind	Reason Mind	Wise Mind
Body Sensations: What do you notice about your body when in this State of Mind?			
Thoughts: What do you notice about your thoughts when in this State of Mind?			
Communication: What do you notice about the way you communicate when in this State of Mind?			
Actions or Action Urges: What do you do or feel like doing when in this State of Mind?			

Find Your Wise Mind in a Crisis

There are short-term and long-term skills you can employ to find your Wise Mind. We will begin with a discussion about using short-term Crisis Survival skills to find Wise Mind when in a difficult or crisis situation with your teen.

Difficult or crisis situations can trigger intense emotions and problem behaviors in your teen. This, of course, has an impact on you as well. Wise Mind becomes more difficult to achieve during and after these events. The first thing to do is to notice your State of Mind. Pay attention to the red flags that might indicate that you are in Emotion or Reason Mind. Recall your observations from the States of Mind worksheet. Being in Wise Mind will help you increase empathy and better problem solve solutions to the crisis.

If you find yourself in Emotion Mind, a break is likely needed. Keep in mind that even a 2- to 5-minute break can be helpful and lessen the impact of Emotion Mind on your decisions and reactions to your teen and the situation. The goal with your break is to focus away from the crisis or difficult situation. This will allow you to slow down and regain perspective. The Crisis Survival skills (including Wise Mind ACCEPTS, Self-Soothe, IMPROVE the Moment, Creative Outlet, and Half-Smile) in the Distress Tolerance module offer ways to take a break. Following, each Distress Tolerance skill is reviewed, with suggestions of ways you can use these skills with a little or a lot of time. When practicing these skills, be mindful and try to only focus on taking a break.

Wise Mind ACCEPTS

The goal of the Wise Mind ACCEPTS skill is to distract from the stressor or crisis (Linehan, 1993b). Distraction will allow your emotions to reduce in intensity and help you move away from Emotion Mind. Each letter in ACCEPTS stands for a way to distract:

	Requires 5 Minutes or Less	Requires More Than 5 Minutes
A—Activities Distract by keeping your mind and body busy	• Check email • Complete a short household task (e.g., empty dishwasher, put clothes away) • Take 10 deep breaths • •	• Exercise • Complete a more involved chore or task (e.g., laundry, vacuum) • Work on an art project • •
C—Comparisons Distract by comparing your situation to other situations that are worse	• Think of ways that you or your teen have improved; remember small changes • Compare your teenager to others you know are doing worse • •	• Talk with other parents about what has worked with their teen • Journal about a time when things were worse; consider things that are going well • •

	Requires 5 Minutes or Less	Requires More Than 5 Minutes
C—Contributing Distract by doing kind things for others	• Send a positive email to a friend or family member • Complete a short chore or task for a family member (e.g., make a bed, pack a lunch) • _____ • _____	• Bake for a friend or your family • Volunteer at the local food pantry • _____ • _____
E—Emotions Distract by creating a new emotion that is different from the old emotion	• Read an inspirational quote • Look at pictures of calming scenery • Listen to an upbeat song • _____ • _____	• Watch a comedy • Read a mystery novel • _____ • _____
P—Push Away Distract by physically or mentally leaving a crisis or problem situation	• Lie in bed for a few minutes • Imagine being someplace tropical or soothing • _____ • _____	• Take a drive • Go to a friend or relative's house • _____ • _____
T—Thoughts Distract by thinking about something that has nothing to do with stressors	• Count to 100 • Look around the room and find an object that starts with every letter of the alphabet • Sing a song in your head • _____ • _____	• Work on a crossword puzzle or Sudoku • Meditate • _____ • _____
S—Sensations Distract from stressors by awakening one of your five senses	• Suck on a strong mint • Smell perfume • _____ • _____	• Take a hot or cold shower • Cook and eat a spicy dish • _____ • _____

Self-Soothe

The Self-Soothe skill means using your five senses to comfort and nurture yourself (Linehan, 1993b).

	Requires 5 Minutes or Less	Requires More Than 5 Minutes
Sight	• Flip through pictures on your cell phone • Notice flowers, trees or other things in nature • •	• Watch a favorite movie or TV show • Look at old family photos • •
Sound	• Listen to a soothing song • Put on the classical music station • •	• Listen to a favorite album • Take a walk or drive and listen for birds or other nature sounds • •
Taste	• Have a piece of chocolate • Drink some tea • •	• Cook and eat a favorite meal • Go to a bakery and buy a treat • •
Touch	• Put on a comfortable sweater or other clothes • Pet your dog, cat or other animal • •	• Take a bubble bath or hot shower • Get a massage • •
Smell	• Put on fragrant lotion • Smell fresh ground coffee • •	• Bake cookies • Cut the lawn • •

IMPROVE the Moment

One way to manage distress with your teen is to focus on positive things (Linehan, 1993b). Here we can remember the skill using the acronym *IMPROVE*.

	Requires 5 Minutes or Less	Requires More Than 5 Minutes
I—Imagery Use your imagination to feel comfortable and safe	• Imagine being someplace soothing, such as the beach or on vacation • Remember a favorite time with family • _____ • _____	• Listen to guided imagery • Meditate about dreams and goals • _____ • _____
M—Meaning Find a purpose or reason for what you are going through	• Consider ways this crisis will help your teen learn and grow • Remind yourself, "Getting through this will make us stronger" • _____ • _____	• Discuss the positives of a difficult situation you're your spouse or a close friend • List parenting lessons that past crises have taught you • _____ • _____
P—Prayer Connect to something greater and open yourself to the moment	• Say a prayer • Read a spiritual quote • _____ • _____	• Attend church • Meditate • _____ • _____
R—Relaxation Help your body feel more comfortable and calm	• Give yourself a neck massage • Stretch • _____ • _____	• Light a candle and cuddle up on the couch • Read a book • _____ • _____
O—One Thing at a Time Focus on one thing	• Tell yourself, "I can get through the next 10 minutes" • Remind yourself, "I only need to deal with today's problems" • _____ • _____	• Take a walk and only focus on what you experience on the walk • Do only one chore or task at a time • _____ • _____

V—Vacation Take a break from your stressors by doing something special	• Drink coffee and read the paper • Listen to a favorite song • •	• Go to a coffee shop and enjoy a new drink • Get a manicure or pedicure • •
E—Encouragement Become your own cheerleader	• Tell yourself, "I can handle this!" • Remind yourself of your strengths as a parent • •	• Make a list of encouraging statements • Write down all the positive things you have done for your teen • •

Creative Outlet

The Creative Outlet skill is about using your emotional energy to be creative. Everyone has a creative side, and you do not have to be a skilled artist to use the Creative Outlet skill. Use this skill to put your emotional energy into creativity and not to get stuck in a crisis or difficult emotions. Examples include drawing, playing an instrument, knitting or cooking.

Half-Smile

Half-Smile is about changing the expression on your face, which has a direct impact on how you feel (Linehan, 1993b). When we experience emotion, our facial expression changes, too. Half-Smile uses this concept to help us manage distress by changing our facial expression. To do a Half-Smile, sit still and relax your face muscles—try not to put an expression on your face. Notice how it feels to have your face relaxed and expressionless. Next, slightly smile and notice how your face feels. Focus on making your face look calm and peaceful (Linehan, 1993b). If it helps, think about something that helps you feel peaceful and joyful. Practice a Half-Smile in non-stressful situations, and try it when in a difficult situation with your teen.

Having a Wise Mind connection with your emotions can help your teen feel supported emotionally, as you can understand and validate emotions. You will also be able to support your teen logistically, as you can help analyze the situation and problem solve a skills plan.

These Crisis Survival skills are helpful in managing Emotion Mind and finding Wise Mind. Remember that although Crisis Survival skills will help you avoid Emotion Mind, the goal is not to be without emotion. Your emotions are useful and needed in a crisis, as they help you empathize and connect with your teen.

If you notice being in Reason Mind, try spending some time noticing and connecting to your emotions. Take a few minutes and feel your body sensations, allowing any emotions to surface. Don't judge or ignore your emotions—just allow them to be there. Use the Feel Your Feelings skill described on the next page to experience your emotions in a Wise Minded way.

Feel Your Feelings

It is normal for you to have your own emotions, thoughts and reactions to your teen's mental health concerns. It is hard to see your child go through a difficult time and not be able to control the way he or she copes with difficulties. Some difficult emotions you might have include:

• Fear or anxiety

• Guilt or shame

• Helplessness

• Sadness

• Anger

• _____

• _____

It can be challenging to navigate the difficult emotions that come with being a parent of a teenager with mental health concerns. Parents can easily end up acting ineffectively with their emotions by either stuffing or sticking to emotions. The Feel Your Feelings skill can help parents find balance by accepting and validating their own emotions so they can connect with Wise Mind.

STUFFING	FEEL YOUR FEELINGS	STICKING

Stuffing

At times, parents try to ignore, stuff, avoid or invalidate their own feelings. A parent may say or think things such as "I shouldn't feel this way," "It's not Ok for me to be so angry (or hurt, scared, etc.)." Sometimes parents do not feel they have time to experience their own emotions or are afraid to think and feel because of all that is going on with their teen. Ignoring, stuffing or avoiding your emotions causes them to build up and eventually trigger Emotion Mind. Invalidating your emotions creates guilt, shame and avoidance of how you are feeling. This, too, makes Emotion Mind more likely, especially under stress or when your teen is in crisis.

Sticking

Parents can also end up on the other end of the dialectic, where they stick to their difficult emotions. Sticking means holding on to emotions—keeping them around. Parents may replay a stressful situation with their teen and experience difficult emotions over and over. Parents can at times get stuck in emotions like anger or fear. This can cause parents to act from Emotion Mind and makes parenting from Wise Mind much more difficult.

Feel Your Feelings

Feel Your Feelings is the middle ground between stuffing and sticking and is an effective emotional coping skill. Emotions are not positive or negative, good or bad, right or wrong. Sometimes we call emotions like sadness or anger "bad" because we dislike them or they feel uncomfortable. However, all emotions are a normal part of being human, and there is no right or wrong way to have emotions. Judging emotions as good or bad can create suffering because we are invalidating our natural human experience, which we cannot change. It is more effective to think of emotions as comfortable or uncomfortable, enjoyable or difficult.

Feel Your Feelings means learning to accept and validate your own emotions. This is an important part of parenting from Wise Mind. Being comfortable and effective with your emotions is also excellent modeling for your teenagers. Remember that acceptance does not mean giving up or wanting things to be the way they are. Instead, acceptance means simply knowing and acknowledging your emotions as they are, which will allows them to pass or become less intense. This helps you to parent from Wise Mind.

Feel Your Feelings means allowing yourself to feel and experience your emotions as they are—without judgment. Feel Your Feelings also means letting your emotions pass when they are ready to pass (Linehan, 1993b).

You can apply Turn the Mind to increase acceptance of your own emotions. (See page 130 for a reminder about Turn the Mind.) The goal is to acknowledge and validate your emotional experience.

Here are some examples of statements that can help you to Feel Your Feelings:

- "It makes sense for me to feel this way."

- "It's Ok for me to be angry (sad, scared, etc.)."

- "This is a difficult time, and I have difficult emotions."

- "Feeling this way does not make me a bad parent."

- "Lots of parents have difficult emotions."

- "I can feel this way and still make effective decisions with my teenager."

- "It is Ok for me to take a break when I am in Emotion Mind."

- _____

- _____

- _____

Skills for Mindful Parenting

Mindfulness skills are essential for parents. Being mindful means having awareness (Linehan, 1993b). This means being able to quiet our minds so that we can notice what is happening inside and what is happening outside of ourselves.

As a parent, mindfulness helps you:

- Make clear and planned decisions.

- Feel less overwhelmed.

- Reduce intense emotions.

- Focus on effective ways to work with your teen.

- Enjoy shared experiences with your teen.

- Notice small, positive changes.

- Validate and accept your teen and yourself.

- Increase patience and acceptance for things you cannot change.

In DBT, there are two sets of Mindfulness skills:

What Skills: Observe, Describe and Participate

The What Skills are what we do to get into Wise Mind (Linehan, 1993b). These skills teach us to connect with the present moment, helping us to gather information about ourselves and those around us. Gathering this information then allows us to make mindful and planned decisions, rather than simply reacting.

How Skills: One-Mindfully, Non-Judgmentally and Effectively

The How Skills are how we use the What Skills to get into Wise Mind (Linehan, 1993b). These skills help us to focus on one thing at a time, avoid judging ourselves and others and focus on acting skillfully in difficult situations.

Observe, Describe & Participate

Observe

Observing means noticing or paying attention. We can notice external events, which include all things in our environment that we experience with our five senses. We can also notice internal events or experiences that are unique to each individual. Internal events include thoughts, body sensations, emotions and urges. When we Observe, we pay attention to external and internal events without holding onto them. This means we notice information and then let it go. Observing means controlling our attention, which involves making the decision to pay attention and not get caught up on one thought, emotion or experience (Linehan, 1993b). Observing means watching our thoughts come and go, like clouds in the sky or waves in the ocean. The goal of Observing is to take a step back and simply notice. Observing allows us to slow down our experience, so we do not get caught in difficult thoughts and emotions.

Describe

When we Describe, we put words on what we noticed (Linehan, 1993b). Using words to Describe what we noticed help us communicate our experience to others and helps us to make sense what is happening. It is important to avoid judgments when we Describe. Use words to describe the facts, and make sure to call a thought a thought, a feeling a feeling, an opinion an opinion, and so on. Using Describe will help you to be on the same page as your partner and your teen. The idea is to notice and Describe the facts as well as your own opinions, feelings or wants.

Participate

Participate means using the information we gathered with Observe and Describe to make effective decisions. When we participate, we become a part of our experience (Linehan, 1993b). We are no longer just noticing, we are now acting. The decisions you make as a parent involve the Participate skill. The idea is to make mindful and Wise Minded decisions. So, rather than reacting to the moment, we are gathering information and making a mindful choice about how we use that information.

Use the Observe, Describe and Participate skills to gain information about yourself, your teen and other parts of your environment to make informed and purposeful decisions. Consider the following example:

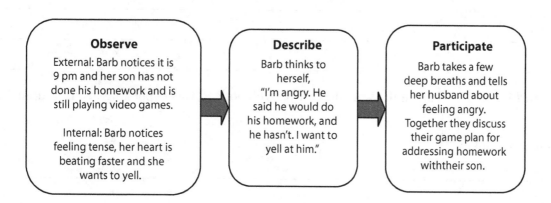

Observe
External: Barb notices it is 9 pm and her son has not done his homework and is still playing video games.

Internal: Barb notices feeling tense, her heart is beating faster and she wants to yell.

Describe
Barb thinks to herself, "I'm angry. He said he would do his homework, and he hasn't. I want to yell at him."

Participate
Barb takes a few deep breaths and tells her husband about feeling angry. Together they discuss their game plan for addressing homework withtheir son.

Notice how using the Observe, Describe and Participate skills helped Barb notice her own reaction so she could make a planned decision on how to act.

Observe, Describe & Participate

Using the Observe, Describe and Participate skills in the moment can be difficult, and building mastery with Mindfulness requires a lot of practice. Looking back at recent situations and recalling what you noticed about how you communicated and acted can help you practice Observe and Describe. This can help you recognize patterns and can remind you to Observe, Describe and Participate when in similar situations.

Think about a recent difficult situation with your teenager. Answer the following questions about this situation.

Observe and Describe—External: Write down what was happening in your environment; include details.

Where were you?

_____

_____

_____

_____

Who was there?

_____

_____

_____

What did you notice with your five senses (e.g., what did you see, hear, touch, smell or taste)?

_____

_____

_____

Observe and Describe—Internal: Write down what you noticed was happening inside you; include details.

What were you thinking?

_____

_____

_____

How did your body feel?

_____

_____

_____

_____

What did you notice about your emotions?

_____

_____

_____

_____

What did you have the urge to do?

_____

_____

_____

Participate: Write down your actions or behaviors; include details.

How did you act; what did you do?

_____

_____

_____

_____

Looking back, how could you have Participated differently (what could you have done differently)?

_____

_____

_____

_____

Try this exercise several times. You can use this worksheet to look back at a difficult situation in the past or use it while you are in a difficult situation in the present. Remember, the goal is to be mindful in the moment and focus on parenting from Wise Mind.

_____

_____

_____

_____

One-Mindfully

One-Mindfully means focusing on only one thing at a time. The goal with this skill is to cut down on overwhelming thoughts and multitasking by focusing on one thing and cutting out distractions.

Here are examples of how to be One-Mindful:

- When talking with your teen, only focus on the conversation.

- When cleaning, only focus on cleaning.

- When taking a shower, only focus on the shower.

- When paying bills, only focus on paying the bills.

- When out with friends, only focus on being with friends.

It is easy for our minds to run amok because there can be so many things to do, think or worry about. The problem is, having our minds in so many places at once actually prevents us from being present with any one thought and keeps us from doing well with any one thing (Linehan, 1993b).

As a parent, One-Mindfully will help you feel more focused and less overwhelmed. This will assist you in parenting from Wise Mind and allow you to feel more capable in difficult situations with your teen. Practicing One-Mindfully will allow you to be in charge of your mind, rather than your mind being in charge of you. This will allow you to focus on and build the relationship with your teenager.

Here are four steps that can help you be One-Mindful:

1. Focus on one thing at a time.
2. Notice when you get distracted or your mind wanders.
3. Re-focus on one thing at a time.
4. Repeat steps 2 and 3 as often as needed.

Practicing the One-Mindful skill is essential. Practice can occur in small steps and can be done any time and any place. Using One-Mindfully simply requires you to be aware of your thoughts and to make a commitment to continually choose where you mind goes (Linehan, 1993b). It is recommended that you start One-Mindfully with a task that is not stressful. For example, practice being One-Mindful when brushing your teeth. Notice all you can about the experience—focus on how the toothbrush feels in your hand, what you taste and how your teeth feel. Being One-Mindful allows you to truly be a part of this experience.

Mindfully brushing your teeth might not seem like a big deal, but consider how you would have filled this time if not focused on brushing your teeth. Many people fill this time with worries about the day and all that needs to be accomplished or replaying a hurtful situation and its emotions. Now consider how many moments like this might exist during your day. This creates a lot of space for difficult emotions, stressful thoughts and activities that are half attended to and prevents you from ever really being in the moment. This sets you up to bring this stress into moments with your teenager, making difficult interactions more difficult or preventing you from seeing and enjoying moments where you could put the relationship first.

Practice One-Mindfully daily by identifying one or two activities to focus your mind on that one thing. Examples could be brushing your teeth, driving to work, cooking a meal or watching TV. These small moments of being One-Mindful will add up and create a Mindful mindset, and you may be inclined to do more things One-Mindfully. One-Mindfully can be frustrating, and some days it will be more difficult. Keep at it, and be gentle with yourself when it does not go as planned.

Non-Judgmentally

Being Non-Judgmental means focusing on the facts and separating our opinions from facts (Linehan, 1993b). Facts are things that can be proven—the who, what, when or where of a situation. Opinions, or judgments, are beliefs or thoughts about the facts. We use judgments easily and without much thought. Using judgment words is often easier than describing facts. The problem is, it's easy for us to see our judgments as facts. When we are Non-Judgmental, we accept things as they are and avoid sticking to our opinions. Having a Non-Judgmental Stance also means identifying our emotions and opinions as emotions and opinions. In other words, a Non-Judgmental Stance means that you do not mistake emotions and opinions for facts.

Remember that it is developmentally typical for teenagers to be self-conscious. This means teens easily perceive judgment, especially from you, the parent. A Non-Judgmental Stance can go a long way in a relationship with a teenager. This is particularly important when a teen struggles with mental health issues like depression or anxiety or difficult urges or behaviors, such as suicidal ideation, self-injury or eating issues. When teens perceive judgment about these sensitive topics, they can get angry or shut down, and this makes it more difficult for them to confide in you or seek your help when they need it.

Practice Non-Judgmentally by avoiding judgment words such as *right*, *wrong*, *good*, *bad*, *smart*, *stupid*, *pretty*, *unfair*, *lazy* or *ambitious*. Keep in mind that *should* is also a judgment word. Remember that judgment words are shorthand for opinion. When using a Non-Judgmental Stance, focus on facts. This does not mean you can't share your opinion or emotions—just make sure you are stating them as such.

Take a look at the following example **not** using a Non-Judgmental Stance.

Event	Parent's Response
Teen acts on urges for self-injury	"This is so stupid! You are so much smarter than this!"

Now look at how this example would change with a Non-Judgmental Stance:

Event	Parent's Response With Non-Judgmental Stance
Teen acts on urges for self-injury	"You acted on your urges to self-injure. I've heard you say that self-injury helps you cope with feeling overwhelmed. I feel scared when this happens, and I believe you can cope in other ways."

In the first example, the teen will likely feel guilt or shame and. despite the parent's urging the teen to be "smarter," the teen may actually feel unable to change. In the second example, the parent states the facts ("You acted on your urges to self-injure. I've heard you say that self-injury helps you cope with feeling overwhelmed"), and uses "I statements" when sharing emotions and opinions. This will likely help the teen understand the parent's perspective while still feeling understood. Remember the goal of a Non-Judgmental Stance is to be accepting and avoid placing your own opinions or evaluations on your teen and his or her choices. This does not mean that you approve of or like your teen's choices; rather, it is about understanding and creating openness to what is.

Effectively

Effectively means doing what works and acting as skillfully as possible (Linehan, 1993b). Being Effective requires being mindful of your goals and making decisions that bring you closer to them. At times, this means letting go of difficult emotions and judgments, which easily get in the way of being Effective.

For parents, Effectively requires parenting decisions that work for your teenager. This means detaching from what a parent "should" do and instead focusing on what you and your teen need. Effectively is not always an easy skill and requires management of many difficult factors, including your teen's mood swings; typical adolescent behaviors; problem behaviors; your own emotions and reactions; and the wants, needs and opinions of other parent(s) and family members.

Acting Effectively requires mindful attention to your *short- and long-term goals*. Your short-term goals will depend on the situation, as you will likely want something specific out of each situation you encounter. For example, if your teen violates curfew, your goal for that situation may be to provide a consequence for breaking the rule. Your long-term goals are the things you want outside of each specific situation—things you want in general for your life, your teen's life or your relationship with your teen. For example, your long-term goal may be building up communication and trust with your teen. Remember that acting Effectively requires you to be mindful of both your short- and long-term goals. So, in addressing a curfew violation with your teen, it will be most effective for you to provide a consequence for breaking the rule while also validating his or her opinions and emotions about the rule and its consequence.

Spending time identifying your goals can help you make decisions and parent more Effectively. Determining how to act Effectively involves considering your options and asking yourself for each option, "Will this bring me closer to or further from my goals?"

Consider the following example:

> Julie's daughter Sarah spent the weekend at her dad's house. Julie learned that Sarah's dad allowed her boyfriend to come over and spend the night. Although Sarah says they did not stay in the same room, Julie is angry and disappointed that this rule, to which both parents had agreed, was broken. Julie thinks about her options. She considers refusing to let Sarah go to her dad's house on the weekends. She also considers breaking a rule that Sarah's dad wanted to show him how unfair it is to change the rules. Julie recognizes that doing these things would take her further from her goal of wanting their divorce to be as conflict-free as possible. Julie decides to take a break by going to lunch with a friend. When she is ready, she calls Sarah's dad to discuss what happened. She tries hard to express her opinion without being aggressive.

In this example, Julie had two goals. Her long-term goal was to make her divorce as conflict-free as possible. Her short-term goal was to have the agreed-on rule of not having Sarah's boyfriend stay the night enforced at both houses. Julie's final solution of calmly talking with Sarah's dad made it more likely that both goals would be met. Julie was able to act Effectively because she was mindful of her goals and let go of emotions and judgments that could have ineffectively influenced her decision.

How you act Effectively will depend on the situation and your goals. A good place to start is by thinking about what you want for your teen and your relationship. Write your long-term goals here:

1. _____

2. _____

3. _____

Be mindful of these goals when a difficult situation arises. Remember to balance these goals with any short-term goals for the situation and let go of emotions and judgments that could get in the way.

Relationship Skills for Parents

Having an Effective relationship with a teenager is a difficult task. This can be particularly difficult for parents, who often bear the brunt of difficult behaviors, emotions and attitudes of a teenager. There can be significant barriers to skillful conversations and effective communication. Although parents cannot control or change how their teenager communicates or responds to attempts at conversations, parents can be mindful in their own communication style.

This section includes several relationship skills that can help parents put their mindful parenting into practice.

GIVE: Put Relationship First

The GIVE skill (Linehan, 1993b) will help you build connected and strong relationship with your teenager. Establishing a foundation of trust and openness will make it more likely that your teen will accept rules, expectations and limits and will assist him or her in coming to you when faced with a difficult situation. This skill can also help you reconnect with your teen as a person and may even help you have fun with him or her.

DEAR MAN: Limit Setting

DEAR MAN is an assertiveness skill (Linehan, 1993b) and will assist you in establishing rules, expectations and limits and in assigning consequences to your teenager. DEAR MAN creates an outline for these difficult conversations and, when used with GIVE, can increase your effectiveness in difficult situations.

Stick to Your Values

Identifying and being mindful of your values will assist you in parenting from Wise Mind and will increase your confidence as a parent. Values can be a guide during difficult times, (Linehan, 1993b) as acting consistently with your values will help you make difficult parenting decisions.

Use these relationship skills together to maximize mindfulness and effectiveness.

GIVE: Put Relationship First

Building a solid relationship with your teenager can make it easier to reinforce limit setting and create a foundation of trust and connectedness. It is easy to fall into the pattern of addressing problem after problem with your teen and to get wrapped up in the many things we have to do during the day. Remember to slow down and at times put the relationship first.

The goal of the GIVE skill is to build and keep healthy relationships (Linehan, 1993b). GIVE is a tool parents can use to put the relationship first. Each letter in GIVE stands for a way we can build and keep healthy relationships:

G—be Gentle

Being Gentle means being kind and respectful. There are many ways we can be Gentle. For example, use a soft tone of voice, make eye contact, use a Non-Judgmental Stance, give a compliment, listen and reflect and use caring feedback.

Being Gentle is important when things are going well *and* when things are not going well in relationships. The idea is to always strive to give respect to your teenager, even when he or she is not giving you respect in return. By having a respectful and gentle attitude and tone, you are modeling ways to build a relationship and are parenting from Wise Mind.

I—act Interested

Act Interested, but not *too* Interested in your teenager. The difficulty here is that teens can often misperceive your interest as being nosy or controlling. Balance is found by showing openness and curiosity of your teen's interests, ideas and opinions while also respecting his or her desire for privacy.

One mistake that parents can make is only acting interested in your teen's problem behaviors, or giving your teen attention and support only when he or she is struggling. When parents do this, they are inadvertently reinforcing problem behaviors. It is thus important to show your teen that you are interested in him or her as a person, rather than being interested only in his or her behaviors.

There are several ways you can act Interested with your teenager. Some examples include to actively listen, do not interrupt, ask questions about his or her opinions or beliefs, make good eye contact, have open body language, be patient when your teen does not want to talk and do not lecture or imply that your teen's thoughts or beliefs are wrong.

V—Validate

To Validate means to show that you understand another person's opinions, feelings, behaviors, wants or point of view. Validation is simply acknowledgment of the other person. The goal of Validation is to express an understanding. Teenagers need a lot of Validation. They are in the process of developing their own identity and sense of self in the world. This can come with uncertainty and insecurity. Validation is a great way to give your teen a sense of security and comfort, and this, of course, is also a wonderful way to build your relationship.

Validation can also be a helpful tool when in conflict with your teen. Validation, or a simple expression of the other person's opinions, emotions or beliefs, can promote a sense of working together, rather than against each other.

Often parents do not use Validation due to a misunderstanding of what Validation means. Parents can have the impression that Validation means you agree with or approve of opinions, beliefs or behaviors. Keep in mind that Validation is simply an expression of understanding, and it does not mean that you agree with or approve of your teenager's feelings, thoughts, opinions, beliefs and behaviors. Validation also does not mean that you give up or are not trying to influence difficult feelings, thoughts, opinions, beliefs or behaviors. Instead, Validation is just acknowledgement and understanding so that you can be on the same page and work together with your teen.

Validation starts with Mindfulness and requires you to pause to Observe and Describe the following:

- What your teen is saying

- His or her facial expressions/body language

- His or her emotions or behaviors

Also consider what might contribute to your teen's feelings, thoughts, opinions, beliefs and behaviors. For instance, what past or present events might cause him or her to have these feelings thoughts, opinions, beliefs or behaviors?

There are many ways to express Validation, and the intention of Validation is to show your teenager that you understand or are trying to understand.

Here are some examples of Validating statements:

- "I understand that you feel really sad today."

- "I notice you are fidgeting a lot. Are you feeling anxious?"

- "Given what you have been through, it makes sense for you to feel this way."

- "I hear you saying _____."

- "It sounds like _____."

- "I can see why you feel/think that way."

There are a few things to avoid when Validating:

- Do not follow your Validation with "but" or "however." Doing so cancels out your Validation. Remember to let your Validation stand on its own. If you want to add something after your Validation, end your Validating statement and add things later.

- Do not personalize. Sometimes parents will try to Validate their teen by sharing a story from their own life or relating the teen's experience to their own. This can actually be invalidating. Remember to make your Validation about your teen's experience; don't make it about you!

E—Easy Manner

Having an Easy Manner means being lighthearted and not taking things too seriously. There is a lot to be serious about as a parent of a teen with mental health concerns. This makes having an Easy Manner all the more important. Having an Easy Manner can help your teenager relate to you and feel relaxed and comfortable. An Easy Manner can also inspire teens to be lighthearted and share their sense of humor with you. This is an important balance to the times when you need to be serious and set limits.

Having an Easy Manner does *not* mean that you take nothing seriously. Use your Wise Mind to help you decide when it is important to be relaxed and lighthearted (Linehan, 1993b). Here are examples of an Easy Manner: Make a joke, smile, focus on the positives, let little things go or do something fun or frivolous.

Remember that the GIVE skill is about building and keeping healthy relationships. The goal here is for you to act in ways that make a connected relationship more likely. Your focus is on your part of the relationship. Remember that you cannot control how your teenager responds. Because your teen is in charge of his or her own behavior, you may not get the response you want, especially right away. If this is the case, give yourself credit for using the GIVE skill and keep trying. Keep in mind that using the GIVE skill with your teen can often make it easier to collaborate and problem solve.

DEAR MAN: Limit Setting

DEAR MAN is an assertiveness skill (Linehan, 1993b) and is helpful to parents when they need to set rules or limits, make a request or say no. DEAR MAN will help you have an outline of how to approach these difficult conversations with your teenager.

D—Describe

Start by discussing the *facts* about the *current* situation (Linehan, 1993b). Be brief when describing, as the goal is simply to get you and your teenager on the same page.

E—Express

Next, express your *feelings* and *opinions* about the facts (Linehan, 1993b). Remember to label feelings as feelings and opinions as opinions. Try to be Non-judgmental and avoid attacking or blaming. "I" statements will help you express. Start a sentence with "I," and remember to own your feelings and opinions and not to blame the other person. For example, "I felt angry when you did not tell me where you were going." Express can also be done briefly. The goal is to tell your teenager what kind of impact his or her actions had on you or to share your opinions about the situation.

A—Assert

Ask for what you want or say no clearly and directly (Linehan, 1993b). Do not be a mind reader or assume that your teenager already knows what you want. Be firm and make sure what you assert is reasonable and understandable.

R—Reinforce

The goal of reinforcement is to make a behavior more likely. This can be done in several ways.

- Share the *positive impacts* of your teen doing what you ask.

    For example, "I would nag less if I knew where you were."

- Share the *negative impacts* of your teen not doing what you ask (often it's more helpful to start with the positive impacts and only share the negative impacts for more serious issues).

    For example, "If you don't tell me where you are going, I will be less likely to say yes when you ask for something."

- Offer your teen a *reward* for doing what you ask. Sometimes rewards can simply be saying thank you and acting grateful. Sometimes rewards can be doing something in return.

    For example, "I might offer you a ride if you tell me where you are going."

- Give a *consequence* for not doing what you ask.

    For example, "You will be grounded next time you don't tell me where you are going."

M—Mindful

It is important to stay calm and focused when you are asserting a rule or limit with your teenager. Remember your goal or why you are using DEAR MAN. Several techniques will help you to be mindful (Linehan, 1993b):

- **Broken Record**

    Keep asking or saying no over and over again. This can also mean being consistent with a rule or consequence. Remember to stay the course and stick to your rule or limit. Sometimes being a Broken Record will mean repeating yourself in the same conversation, and sometimes it will mean repeating yourself in several separate conversations.

- **Ignore**

    Do not respond to threats, disrespect or verbal attacks, as doing so can distract from your goal of setting a limit. End the conversation if you need to, but do not get distracted by a difficult reaction from your teen.

- **Take a Break**

    Sometimes difficult conversations can trigger Emotion Mind.
    Notice if you or your teen is in Emotion Mind and take a break.
    Remember, you can always come back to the conversation later.

A—Act confident

You might not always feel confident when asserting yourself, especially when your teen has a difficult reaction. Act confident and gentle by making eye contact, speaking clearly and not yelling. Do not talk too fast or call names, and take a break if you notice being in Emotion Mind. Remember to speak with confidence but not condescension.

N—Negotiate

Teenagers can respond well to a compromise. Consider ways to meet in the middle and be willing to give in on some things or adjust your rules or limits if it is appropriate. Be willing to work with your teen and try to view things as your being a team that needs to work together. Ask your teen what he or she thinks rules or limits should be, and discuss ways to find a middle ground.

Once a rule or limit has been set, use the CARES skill (page 163) to be consistent and maintain this expectation.

Stick to Your Values

Values are things that are important to you (Linehan, 1993b). Values can be a guide during difficult times, and living in a way that is consistent with your values increases self-respect and promotes a sense of contentment. This is particularly helpful in parenting a teenager.

Each person has his or her own set of values, and your teen is developing his or her own idea of values. Sticking to your values does not mean forcing your values onto your teen, but rather for you to know and parent from your own sense of what is important. This will also encourage your teen to develop his or her own sense of what is important.

Here are some examples of values. Circle what you value, and add your own:

• Family	• Education	• Sports	• Health	• Fun	• Communication
• Spirituality	• Religion	• Adventure	• Safety	• Freedom	• Achievement
• Friends	• Love	• Challenge	• Charity	• Rules	• Individuality
• Peace	• Honesty	• Hard work	• Technology	• Privacy	• Openness
• Cleanliness	• Creativity	• Sobriety	• Career	• Art/music	• Kindness
• Teamwork	• Trust	• Knowledge	• Loyalty	• Money	• Responsibility

• _____   • _____

• _____   • _____

• _____   • _____

Knowing and living in a way that is consistent with your values will help you to be a happy and fulfilled person. It is also important to consider how your values can be brought to life in your parenting.

Think about what is important to you as a parent. Consider what kind of a parent you want to be. Write down qualities you think it is important for a parent to have:

_____

_____

_____

_____

_____

Sticking to your values means living in a way that is consistent with what is important to you (Linehan, 1993b). We often lose sight of our values when experiencing intense situations or emotions. Remember your values and be mindful of ways to bring your values into interactions with your teens. Also remember not to force your values on your teen, as he or she will have his or her own unique set of values. Your teen's values might be different from yours. Remember not to judge or act from Emotion Mind if your values differ.

Self-Care

Self-Care means engaging in behaviors that contribute to personal well-being and health. Self-Care promotes wellness in several areas, including physical health, mental/emotional health and spiritual health.

Self-Care is important for many reasons. Self-Care reduces Emotional vulnerability. Emotional vulnerability means being at risk for difficult emotions. When you are emotionally vulnerable, daily stressors have a greater impact, and coping with them becomes more difficult.

A Self-Care routine helps us balance the effects of emotional and physical stressors. In other words, when we regularly engage in Self-Care, we are rejuvenating our physical and emotional resources, which are depleted by daily life events and stress. Regular Self-Care can prevent or limit physical and emotional problems in the long term.

Self-Care as the parent of a teenager is especially important for the following reasons:

- Modeling Self-Care can help your teen learn and use Self-Care skills.

- As a parent, you will have difficult emotions and reactions to your teen's behaviors and mental health. It is important that you care for yourself so that you have the resources you need in the process.

- When you have good Self-Care, you will more likely to parent from Wise Mind. Poor Self-Care can easily lead to Emotion Mind. Remember that being in Wise Mind will assist you in making effective decisions as a parent.

- Self-Care will help you balance parenting responsibilities and the demands of daily life.

PLEASE: Care for your Physical Health

The PLEASE skill is focused on physical Self-Care. There is a strong connection between your body and mind. Tending to your physical health will reduce emotional vulnerability (Linehan, 1993b) and promote mental health. Each letter in the PLEASE skill stands for a way to take care of your physical health. Keep in mind that Self-Care is not about being perfect, but rather the goal is to take small steps toward improved health.

PL—treat PhysicaL illness

Treating PhysicaL illness means taking care of yourself when you are sick and caring for underlying medical conditions. Here are some examples of ways to treat PhysicaL illness:

- See a doctor when ill
- Take medicines as prescribed
- Get extra sleep when sick

- _____
- _____
- _____

E—balanced Eating

Eat so that you have enough energy to get through the day. Don't eat too much or too little. Here are some examples of ways to have balanced Eating:

- Eat at least one vegetable at every meal
- Eat mindfully
- Have fruit as a snack
- Plan out meals for the week
- Drink enough water

- _____
- _____
- _____

A—Avoid mood-altering drugs

Stay away from alcohol and street drugs and only take prescriptions as the doctor prescribed. Limit caffeine and avoid tobacco. Here are additional suggestions for Avoiding mood-altering drugs:

- Only have one soda or coffee each day
- See a doctor for help quitting smoking

- Remove alcohol from the home and have only on special occasions

- _____
- _____

S—balanced Sleep

Try to get the right amount of sleep for you. Do not sleep too much or too little. Here are suggestions for ways to get balanced Sleep:

- Go to bed and wake up at the same time every day
- Make sure your bed is comfortable

- Don't read or watch TV in bed • Nap only when really needed • Don't have caffeine after noon

- _____
- _____
- _____

E—balanced Exercise

Try to get some exercise every day. Here are suggestions for ways to get balanced Exercise:

- Take the stairs instead of the elevator
- Take a short walk every day
- Play a sport

- Park at the end of the parking lot
- Do yard work or shovel
- Join a gym

- _____
- _____
- _____

PLEASE Evaluation

Consider your strengths and weaknesses with the PLEASE skill. Identify one small step you could take in each area of PLEASE.

	What I Do Well	What I Need to Work On	A Small Step I Could Take in This Area
treat **P**hysica**L** illness			
balanced **E**ating			
Avoid mood-altering drugs			
balanced **S**leep			
balanced **E**xercise			

Self-Care: Beyond PLEASE

Remember that Self-Care is about acting in ways that promote physical, emotional and spiritual well-being. Here are some additional ways to improve Self-Care.

Limit stress:

- Say no to things you do not have to take on.

- Prioritize your to-do list, and focus on only one item at a time.

- Ask for help if needed.

- _____

- _____

- _____

Have and use a support system:

- Talk to other parents.

- Go on regular dates with your partner or spouse.

- Do enjoyable activities with your friends.

- Attend support groups for parents.

- _____

- _____

- _____

Make time for yourself each day:

- Set aside 5 to 10 minutes to do something you enjoy.

- Take a nightly walk.

- Use Self-Soothe.

- Relax daily.

- _____

- _____

- _____

Connect with your spiritual side:

- Pray

- Meditate

- Join a religious group or class

- _____

- _____

- _____

Self-Care: A Family Affair

Self-Care is about making decisions for your health and wellness. Each individual is responsible for his or her own Self-Care, and this includes teenagers. Remember that you cannot make your teen change his or her Self-Care choices. However, there are ways that you influence your teen and family's Self-Care.

Model Self-Care

Teenagers are more likely to do what they see than what they are told. One of the most influential ways to promote Self-Care with your teenager is by having good Self-Care yourself. Small steps with your own Self-Care can improve your whole household's Self-Care. For example, if you take steps toward improved eating, you may not buy junk food and will be likely to have fruits and vegetables readily available. This will make healthy food available and junk food unavailable not only to you but to your teen as well. Plus, your positive change can inspire and motivate change in others.

Create Family Goals

Sit down with your teen and other family members to have a conversation about Self-Care. Have a positive and non-judgmental approach, and ask your family about Self-Care strengths and weaknesses. Discuss reasonable goals to work on as a family, ways you can hold each other accountable and ways to encourage each other when you hit low spots in making change.

Make family goals *reasonable*. Make sure that you can accomplish your goal. If in doubt, make the goal easier rather than harder. Remember that you can always make a goal more challenging, and accomplishing a goal can motivate you to keep going.

Break your big goals into *small steps,* and focus on one step at a time. It may take more time to achieve your goal but will ensure lasting change.

Make family goals *measurable*. Having a way to measure success with goals will help you recognize change and give you a concrete step on which to focus. An example of measurement is having a targeted number of times each day or week you would like to accomplish your goal.

Use the CARES Skill to Create Consistency

Review the next section to learn the CARES skill, which will help you create consistency with your Self-Care goals.

Review this example and complete the following worksheet to set Self-Care goals with your family.

Goal: Improve balanced Exercise as a family.
>   **Small Step #1:** Take a walk as a family one time each week.
>   **Accountability:** We will mark a star on the calendar for each day a walk is taken, and if we have at least three stars by the end of the month, we'll go out for a special family dinner.
>   **Encouragement:** We will tell each other "you can do it!" if we don't feel like following through.
>   **Small Step #2:** Start parking at the end of the parking lot when we go to the store.
>   **Accountability:** Every evening, tell each other if we parked at the end of a parking lot that day.
>   **Encouragement:** Send each other positive notes or texts.

Family Goals for Self-Care

Goal #1: _____

Small Step #1: _____

Accountability: _____

_____

Encouragement: _____

_____

Small Step #2: _____

Accountability: _____

_____

Encouragement: _____

_____

Goal #2: _____

Small Step #1: _____

Accountability: _____

_____

Encouragement: _____

_____

Small Step #2: _____

Accountability: _____

_____

Encouragement: _____

_____

CARES: A Skill for Consistency

Consistency is very important when parenting teenagers. Consistency creates predictability, safety and structure, which provides balance to the risk taking and desire for autonomy typical of teenagers. Consistency is key when setting and reinforcing limits and boundaries. Inconsistency prevents rules from sticking and creates confusion and more difficulty for both you and your teen. Consistency is also key in creating change. New changes and skills need to be practiced and used daily to stick.

CARES is a skill that can help to create consistency. Remember that although teenagers may resist routine, rules and change, being consistent is actually a way that parents show care.

C—Commitment

Consistency starts by making a commitment. Think about and write down your goals and reasons for wanting a new change. Make an inner commitment to create this change, and when you encounter difficulties, remind yourself of why you chose this change in the first place.

A—Accountable

Be held accountable. Identify support people that you can report your progress to and work with others (or yourself) to set rewards or consequences for following through with your new change. Consider putting your goals in writing and keep track of how often you are following through.

R—Reminders + Routine

Reminders will keep your new change fresh in your mind, making it more likely that you will follow through. There are many ways to create reminders about your new routine. Examples include setting an alarm on your phone, putting Post-It notes on the bathroom mirror or fridge or having a support person offer you verbal reminders of your new change.

Make your new change routine. Consider ways to attach new changes to existing routines. For example, if you are inconsistent in taking medication, put your medication by your toothbrush and plan to take it right before brushing your teeth each morning. Adding something to an existing routine can make the new task easier to remember, and over time it will become its own routine. Follow through with your new change at the same time every day. The key to lasting change is practice, practice, practice.

E—Encouragement

Change is hard! Be your own cheerleader and give yourself lots of encouragement and credit for working toward something new. Tell yourself, "I can do this," or "Way to go!" Consider putting up Post-Its with encouraging statements in places you will see, or read inspirational stories or quotes from time to time.

S—Small Steps

Start small and create achievable goals. Once you have made progress on one small step, you can then add an additional step. Lasting change often happens slowly over time, and focusing on only one small step can make change more doable.

My Teen Is in DBT: Tips for Parents

Here are some tips for parents who have teens in therapy.

DBT Programs

DBT programs generally involve both individual therapy and group skills training. Traditionally, teens learn DBT skills in a group setting and use individual therapy to identify ways to apply the skills to situations in their day-to-day life. Sometimes teens only have individual therapy and learn DBT skills in a one-on-one setting.

Safety First

DBT therapists see safety as the number one priority. If your teen struggles with self-injury or suicidal thoughts, his or her therapist will help your teen use DBT skills to be safe. In therapy, safety issues are addressed first, and it's the therapist's responsibility to make sure your teen is safe when he or she leaves the therapy session. Ask your teen and his or her therapist how you can help with safety plans at home.

Respect Your Teen's Need for Privacy

Like adults, teens are more likely to benefit from therapy when they know it is a safe and private place to talk about difficult thoughts and feelings. Although it makes sense for you to be curious about your teen's therapy, remember to give your teen privacy and do not pry about what he or she does in therapy.

Change Can Take Time

There are a lot of variables that can make change a slow process. Some teens might need time to build a relationship with a therapist and/or peers in a therapy group before they start to open up. Some teens are not yet ready to change and may need some time in therapy to think about the pros and cons of changing. Changing habits requires a lot of practice, and change can happen in small steps. Be patient and mindful of small change.

Communication with the Therapist

It is Ok to touch base with your teen's therapist, and sharing your thoughts or insights can be helpful. Sometimes therapists will hear what you have to say but won't share a lot in return. This is because the therapist is trying to make sure your teen has privacy. Sometimes you can join a therapy session. During these sessions, it is Ok to ask your teen and his or her therapist about how you can help.

When to Get Your Own Therapy

Sometimes parents need their own place to talk about difficult emotions, thoughts and behaviors. You should see your own therapist if you notice that your needs are not being met by the parent elements of a DBT program. If you are having difficulty going to work or managing tasks at home, are having difficulty in relationships or are experiencing suicidal ideation or self-harm, you should see your own therapist.

Part Three

Therapist's Guide

Providing DBT for Teens

Providing DBT for teens is a fun, fulfilling and challenging endeavor. Teenagers bring a unique perspective and, of course, lots of energy. Working with teens requires the therapist to have a unique set of skills and approaches, and therapists need to constantly adjust to meet clients where they are. The therapist section of this book begins with themes and principles that will guide and enhance your work with teens in DBT. This includes:

- Information about DBT's format, targets and functions and discussion of how DBT's structure guides and ensures the stability of a DBT program

- Descriptions of the developmental tasks of adolescence, including tips on how you can support healthy development

- Explanations of the adolescent-specific Dialectical Dilemmas and insights to help you find balance in addressing these conflicts

- Illumination of the benefits of teaching with activities and skills to help you have experiential attitude and approach

Then, practical information and tools are taught to help you run an effective and active therapy environment. These include:

- Activities to teach skills in each of the four skill modules

- Example documents to work with teens and run an adolescent DBT group

The skills and information presented in the therapist section is geared toward a traditional DBT program consisting of a skills group, individual therapy, phone coaching and DBT consultation. However, this information can enhance any therapist's work with adolescents and can be applied to traditional and adapted DBT settings, as well as non-DBT therapy programs and individual therapy.

The goal of the therapist section of this book is to provide basic and essential information and tips for practical application in doing DBT with adolescents. Therapists are referred to Marsha Linehan's original books, *Cognitive-Behavioral Treatment of Borderline Personality Disorder* (1993a) and *Skills Training Manual for Treating Borderline Personality Disorder* (1993b) for a more extensive description of the theory and practice of DBT. *Dialectical Behavior Therapy for Suicidal Adolescents* (Miller, Rathus, Linehan, 2007) is also recommended for lengthy explanations of how DBT's theory and practice was originally adapted for adolescents.

DBT Program Format, Targets & Functions

DBT's structure is an essential element, as it promotes a consistent and effective program. The structure of an adolescent DBT program is similar to that of a DBT program for adults. One of the biggest differences between the two is the inclusion of parents in a program for adolescents. This section includes program structure basics. Readers are referred to Marsha Linehan's book *Cognitive-Behavioral Treatment of Borderline Personality Disorder* (1993a) for more detailed descriptions. Following are descriptions of DBT's format, treatment targets and functions.

DBT Program Format

DBT programs involve four components:

1. Group skills training
2. Individual therapy
3. Phone coaching
4. Therapist consultation

Group Skills Training. A DBT skills group is the primary place clients learn DBT skills (Linehan, 1993a). In each skills group, clients participate in skill lessons and activities to help them learn the skills and gain an understanding of how to apply them to daily life. Skills groups typically include weekly homework to assist clients in practicing DBT outside of therapy. DBT skills groups additionally include Diary Card review to assist clients in recognizing areas in which they can apply skills.

In the book *Dialectical Behavior Therapy with Suicidal Adolescents* (2007), Miller, Rathus and Linehan discuss having at least one parent attend each skills group with his or her teenager. The intention is for parents to learn DBT skills so that they can be of greater assistance to the teen in applying skills at home. An added bonus of including parents in skills groups is helping parents recognize and problem solve their role in the creation or persistence of mental health concerns.

There are also adapted DBT models in which only teenagers attend skills group, and their parents are included in other ways, such as separate multi-family education groups, inclusion in individual therapy sessions, family therapy or individual check-ins with the teen and DBT therapist(s). There are several benefits to having a teen-only skills group. First, teen clients tend to have a higher level of disclosure and openness, which helps them apply DBT skills to real-life issues. Second, teen-only skill groups promote independence and can increase a teen client's investment in and motivation for change. Third, teens are more likely to offer both validating and challenging feedback to their peers. Lastly, teens with parents who are unable to attend a skills group still get the therapy they need.

If parents are not included in DBT skill groups, therapists are strongly encouraged to offer alternatives to assist parents in learning and applying DBT at home. A parent only multi-family education groups are an effective way to involve parents outside of a DBT skills group. The parent section of this book can be used as curriculum for parent only multi-family education groups. The goal is to assist parents in learning and applying DBT to their own parenting. Parent-only education groups also have benefits: They allow parents to disclose difficult thoughts and feelings about parenting a mentally ill teenager as well as give and receive validating and challenging feedback from other parents. Frequency of these groups can vary, but it is recommended that they are held no less than once monthly.

Whether parents attend DBT skills groups or multi-family psychoeducation groups, therapists are encouraged to be mindful of and create balance between including parents and protecting a teen client's therapeutic privacy. Readers are referred to the section of this book on the Dialectical Dilemma "Parental Involvement vs. Therapeutic Privacy" on page 178 for more information about how to strike this balance.

Individual Therapy. Individual therapy is recommended once per week and is an indispensable partner to DBT skill groups. Individual therapy is the place where clients learn to generalize their skill use and increase effectiveness in applying DBT skills to bigger life concerns and thought and behavioral patterns (Linehan, 1993a). Individual therapy allows for in-depth Diary Card review. Using the Diary Card as a therapeutic tool provides structure that generally improves focus and effectiveness in an individual therapy session. In traditional DBT models, individual therapy guides the therapeutic process, and coordination between skills group and individual therapy is essential.

Parents can be invited into an individual therapy session to directly address teen-parent issues. In these cases, it is recommended that the therapist support and reinforce the teen client's attempts to independently resolve parent concerns. Joining individual therapy sessions can additionally provide parents with psychoeducation on mental illness and DBT. It is important to remember that although parents can join individual therapy sessions, the teen is the focus of therapy. Avoid sharing private information, and encourage the teen to guide sessions that include parents. If the therapeutic needs of the parent or family exceed the scope of a teen's individual therapy, it is recommended that referrals are made for family therapy or individual therapy for the parent.

Phone Coaching. In traditional DBT programs, clients are given access to their therapist 24/7 (Linehan, 1993a). Clients are encouraged to call their therapist outside session in the following situations:

1. The client is in crisis and having difficulty applying skills. A call to a therapist is intended to assist the client in problem solving the situation. This increases skill use and can prevent crisis behaviors.
2. There is positive news or skill success. Clients are encouraged to make a phone call to report positive progress to their therapists.
3. There is a therapeutic rift between the client and therapist. Clients are encouraged to address relationship concerns to prevent them from building and interfering with therapy.

There are alternatives to 24/7 phone access. In adapted DBT programs, therapists may be available during the therapist's working hours for coaching calls. Outside of working hours, clients are provided phone numbers for crisis lines. Although the individual who answers the crisis line may not be DBT trained, he or she is trained in crisis management and can assist clients in getting their needs met until their next therapy session. In traditional or adapted DBT programs, clients are expected to receive emergency services if they are unsafe and their therapist is not available to take their call.

Consultation. Clinical consultation is often the glue that holds a DBT program together. Consultation groups are intended to offer support to the therapist and address both client and therapist issues (Linehan, 1993a). Remember that therapists sometimes engage in therapy-interfering behaviors. Consultation is a place where these behaviors can be identified and problem solved. Consultation helps maintain therapist motivation and promotes continued learning and development of clinical skills.

DBT Treatment Targets

DBT is a hierarchical treatment, meaning that the therapist attends to some issues before others. Treatment targets, in order of importance, are as follows (Linehan, 1993a):

1. Safety issues (such as suicidal ideation and self harm)

2. Therapy interfering-behaviors (such as absenteeism, refusal to participate, creating conflict in skills group)

3. Quality of life–interfering behaviors (such as substance abuse, impulsive behaviors like shoplifting, poor self-care)

4. Acquisition of DBT skills (in each of the four DBT modules: Mindfulness, Distress Tolerance, Emotion Regulation and Interpersonal Effectiveness).

The treatment hierarchy exists to guide therapists and clients by addressing the most important issues first. This structure creates stability and predictability and ensures that barriers (such as safety issues, therapy and quality of life–interfering behaviors) are removed, which enhances the acquisition of skills (Linehan, 1993a).

The treatment hierarchy is particularly helpful to therapists who provide DBT to teenagers. Teens can get distracted easily. Their focus on peer relationships and events at home and school can often lead to confusion about which behavior or issue to address first. Therapists are reminded to follow the treatment hierarchy in navigating individual and group sessions. Teens can additionally be socialized to identify and address the hierarchy independently. This supports the teen's developmental task of autonomy and maximizes the impact that treatment can have on the individual teen client as well as a skills group.

Treatment Functions

DBT's treatment functions capture the purpose of a DBT program and, again, act as a guide for treatment. DBT provides five treatment functions (Linehan, 1993a):

1. **Improving motivation to change.** Therapists need to meet the client where he or she is and recognize disruptions in the motivation to change (Linehan, 1993a). DBT can be a long-term process and requires a lot of work. For this reason, mindfulness of a client's motivation to change is important in ensuring he or she can see the therapy process to the end. Therapists can assist in improving motivation for change by identifying and addressing client thoughts or behaviors that may impact a commitment to DBT. It is recommended that therapists highlight and reinforce even small steps toward change and through pattern recognition assist the client in identifying the pros of changing and the cons of not changing. Additionally, discussing the client's life goals and aspirations can spark motivation and recognition of how a DBT program can move him or her closer to these goals. Improving the motivation to change is primarily an individual therapy task. However, therapists facilitating a skills group can also be mindful of opportunities to increase the motivation to change.

2. **Increasing capabilities and skills.** DBT is a skills-focused treatment, so addressing skill deficits and increasing a client's capabilities and skill use is a primary goal of a DBT program (Linehan, 1993a). Clients are taught each skill and how to apply it to daily life events and stressors. A skills group is the primary place this function is met. However, individual therapy and phone coaching can also play a role in teaching skills.

3. **Ensuring skill generalization.** DBT assists clients in learning and using skills. The next step is applying skills to deeper thought and behavioral patterns (Linehan, 1993a). This means that the client can apply the same skill to a wide variety of situations and recognize what type of situation calls for what type of skill. Individual therapy, skills group and phone coaching are each places where skill generalization can occur.

4. **Structuring the environment to support clients, family and therapists.** DBT's structure exists in the formats of treatment, the treatment hierarchy and in the treatment functions (Linehan, 1993a). In the beginning, DBT's structure is detailed and can be overwhelming. However, the structure of a DBT program exists to provide support to the client, family and therapist. DBT's structure has been well thought out and provides an outline for treatment. As noted previously, this provides an element of predictability and safety, both for the client and the therapist. This makes providing services to an intense population less intimidating and more accessible.

5. **Enhancing capabilities and motivation of therapists.** Clinical consultation and training exist in a DBT program to ensure that therapists are motivated for treatment and have the skills they need to put this motivation into action (Linehan, 1993a). Consultation also allows therapists to recognize their therapy-interfering behaviors and address counter-transference. This ensures the most effective therapy program.

Similarly to the treatment targets, the treatment functions can be a guiding light to therapists in work with teenagers. By being mindful of the treatment functions, therapists can recognize ways to balance being strict and lenient and to encourage independence while also providing support.

Adolescent Developmental Tasks

Each stage of development brings with it new skills and abilities. During each stage of development, these new skills and abilities are difficult, and learning them is cumbersome. The developmental tasks of adolescence can bring confusion and frustration to the teen's life and can have a significant impact on those around them. The difficult behaviors demonstrated by teens in a DBT group can fall along a spectrum of developmentally typical to more extreme expressions of developmental tasks.

It is important for therapists to recognize the developmental tasks of adolescence. A teenager will not come to therapy saying, "I'm learning about intimacy and self-identity in relationships," but will become focused on fitting in with his or her group peers and be on the lookout for indications of what group peers think about him or her. Recognizing how teen behaviors are typical of adolescence will help a therapist know what is beyond typical development. For instance, it is typical for a teen to be concerned if group peers accept him or her, but it is not typical for a teen to have a panic attack in anticipation of possible rejection. Reviewing the developmental tasks of adolescence and the ways they come to life in a therapy group will help you differentiate developmentally typical behaviors from behaviors that suggest a greater mental health concern.

Additionally, therapists are highly encouraged to allow these developmental tasks to take center stage and guide the treatment of teenagers. Teen clients will only benefit from support and attention to the development of new skills and abilities, and therapy offers a unique and important environment for movement through this developmental stage.

Adjusting to Brain Development

Teenagers are undergoing significant changes in brain development. Teens are becoming better at reasoning and can consider many options and think about things hypothetically (McNeely & Blachard, 2010). They are acquiring the new skill of thinking abstractly and can be focused on ideas like trust and loyalty. One of the most impactful cognitive developments in this stage is metacognition, or the ability to think about thinking. Teenagers are developing the ability to think about having thoughts and emotions. This leads to greater introspection and is responsible for the egocentrism often seen in adolescence. Additionally, metacognition and the ability to think hypothetically lead to the ability to take the perception of others (McNeely & Blachard, 2010). This contributes to an over-focus on how others may perceive them, which can compound insecurity or self-consciousness. Although teens have new cognitive skills, the area of the brain responsible for planning and identifying long-term consequences is not yet fully developed, so although they can see the abstract, they are still not very skilled with planning and thinking ahead.

Therapists can support adjustment to enhanced cognitive development by teaching the theory behind DBT and using a discussion format to help teens consider ways DBT applies to daily life. Additionally, teaching with activities can help teenagers better translate the abstract concepts of some DBT skills into concrete action. Therapists can also help teenagers with planning ahead and recognizing consequences by asking them to consider the pros and cons of decisions already made, as well as decisions yet to be made. Therapists can use Socratic questioning to help teens recognize the impact of their own decisions.

Establishing an Identity

Teenagers are figuring out who they are. This involves integrating the opinions of others into one understanding of themselves . Identify formation involves asking and looking for the answers to questions such as, "Who am I?" "What is possible for me?" "Who will I become?" "What is important to me" (McNeely & Blachard, 2010)? Changes in brain development open the door for identity restructuring, and adolescents are exploring who they are in terms of abstract concepts rather than the more concrete ones of hobbies or material possessions. Additionally, teenagers must incorporate their changing bodies and variety of social roles into their self-identity (McNeely & Blachard, 2010). The goal of this task is to have a clear sense of one's own opinions, values and beliefs, be comfortable in one's own body and know who one is in relation to others.

Therapists can support the development of self-identity by allowing and promoting a sense of cohesion plus individuality in DBT skills group and individual therapy. Therapists can express curiosity and facilitate discussion of a teen's opinions, beliefs, values and behaviors. By asking questions and guiding discussions, therapists are promoting a more cohesive sense of self. Additionally, reinforcement of boundaries with skills group peers can assist teens in recognizing how they are similar and different from others.

Establishing Autonomy

Teenagers are working on independence and finding their own way in the world. Building autonomy requires them to maintain social connections (including those with parents), while also becoming more self-reliant. Autonomy involves self-directed decision making, developing a belief that one can function independently, and creating a sense of individuation from parents (McNeely & Blachard, 2010). Increased autonomy does not mean detachment from parents or outside support. Instead, autonomy is about creating a sense of self as independent from others. This means making their own decisions and living by their own sense of what is right and wrong. Teens are working on being less dependent on their parents and often push their parents and family away. This pushing away is about making room for their own decisions and acting independently. The goal of increased autonomy is being prepared for an adult role in the world.

Autonomy is one of the primary developmental tasks of adolescence, and therapists can foster autonomy easily throughout a DBT skills group and individual therapy. Therapists are encouraged to put teen clients in an active role in as many elements of a DBT program as possible. This active role is supported with structure, limits and guidance by the therapist. The therapist's goal is to shape the skills group to be self-functioning and for the therapist have a supportive role the majority of the time.

Practicing Intimacy and Closeness in Relationships

Teenagers are focused on and interested in peer relationships and are finding new ways to be intimate with others (McNeely & Blachard, 2010). This includes emotional and sexual intimacy. Often this intimacy occurs with platonic friendships but can also include a significant other. This area of development will be prevalent in DBT skills groups.

Although the goal of skills groups is to teach skills, teenagers will often be more focused on their peers and relationships with them than they are DBT skills. Therapists can support this developmental task by helping teens create connections with peers while also having boundaries and a focus on their own needs. An active teaching approach can also create opportunities for teens to join with each other around learning and using DBT skills. Immediately addressing glorification of ineffective behaviors and promoting encouragement around Effective coping can also foster a healthy approach to building peer relationships.

Adjusting to a Developing and Changing Body

Teenagers experience significant changes in their bodies, and this requires some adjustment. Teens often become over-focused on their appearance (McNeely & Blachard, 2010) and the appearance of others. This can cause them to be self-conscious or have difficulty figuring out how to dress or how they want to appear to others. Hormonal changes additionally impact a teenager's mood, and rapidly changing moods are typical.

Therapists must expect mood fluctuations and differentiate them from mental health problems such as depression or anxiety. Therapists can also create a safe and consistent therapy environment to minimize the impacts of self-consciousness.

Dialectical Dilemmas

Remember that a Dialectical Dilemma occurs when one feels stuck between two ideas that seem opposite to each other (Linehan, 1993a). Having a solid understanding of Dialectical Dilemmas will assist therapists in seeing and working Effectively with them as they occur in therapy. The therapist's goal is to help teen clients and their parents find balance by incorporating elements from both sides of the dialectic.

This book discusses the three adolescent-specific Dialectical Dilemmas first identified by Miller, Rathus and Linehan (2007) in their book, *Dialectical Behavior Therapy with Suicidal Adolescents*. Practical information is provided about how to engage Effectively with these Dialectical Dilemmas.

Fostering Independence vs. Giving Support

Therapists can strike a balance on this dialectic by encouraging clients to be the leader of their own treatment while also offering support, problem solving and advocacy. Therapists facilitating a skills group have a difficult task with this dialectic, as balance needs to be struck for each individual client but also for the group as a whole. The goal is to create a group that functions collaboratively while also allowing individual group members space to make independent choices and an identity that is connected to but separate from the group.

Being Strict vs. Being Lenient

Finding balance with this dialectic means having expectations, rules or limits while also being flexible. This requires the therapist to have an active role in creating a therapeutic structure that focuses on DBT's targets and functions while also empowering clients to accomplish these tasks in their own way.

Allowing Developmentally Typical Behaviors vs. Addressing Problem Behaviors

Finding balance with this dialectic means letting teenagers practice their developmental tasks while taking seriously behaviors that are beyond what one would expect developmentally. For therapists, this means not pathologizing typical teenage behavior while also addressing problem behaviors.

This book includes a new Dialectical Dilemma that often presents challenges to therapists working with teenagers in DBT:

Involving Parents vs. Protecting Client Privacy

Finding balance with this dialectic means actively engaging and promoting change with parents while also ensuring that teenagers have a private and safe therapeutic environment.

The developmental tasks of adolescence are woven throughout discussion of these Dialectical Dilemmas. Therapists are encouraged to continually be mindful of supporting the developmental tasks of increased independence and autonomy, development of self-identity, relationship building and adjustment to body and brain changes.

Developmental Tasks vs. Problem Behaviors

DEVELOPMENTALLY TYPICAL BEHAVIORS	BALANCE	PROBLEM BEHAVIORS

Allow Developmentally Typical Behaviors. On this end of the dialectic, therapists are allowing room for teen clients to practice developmental tasks. This means mindfulness of and flexibility for autonomy, identity development, creating closeness in relationships and adjustment to body and brain changes. Mistakes that therapists can make on this end of the dialectic are providing too much room for difficult behaviors and not creating enough structure and accountability for meeting treatment expectations. Additionally, therapists can misidentify mental health concerns by writing problem behaviors off as developmentally typical (Miller, Rathus, Linehan, 2007). This contributes to under-diagnosing and lost opportunities to apply DBT skills to problem areas.

Address Problem Behaviors. Problem behaviors are extreme forms of developmentally typical behaviors. Problem behaviors create harm or significant consequences for the teen and/or his or her family. Therapists on this end of the dialectic identify and address problem behaviors and encourage application of DBT skills to problem solve the behaviors. Mistakes that therapists can make on this end of the dialectic include over-pathologizing by mistaking developmentally typical behaviors as a symptom of a greater mental health concern (Miller, Rathus, Linehan, 2007). For example, the moodiness that is typical of adolescence could be mistaken as the affective dysregulation seen in Borderline Personality Disorder. This can lead to over-diagnosing or inaccurate mental health diagnosing. Additionally, therapists may mistakenly over-attend to behaviors or struggles that are developmentally typical. This can also become a lost opportunity to apply DBT skills to true mental health concerns.

Balance. Balancing this dialectic means cultivating an environment that is receptive to the developmental tasks of adolescence while also identifying and addressing behaviors that are beyond typical development (Miller, Rathus, Linehan, 2007). This requires frequent consultation to identify mental health concerns without pathologizing behaviors typical of adolescence. Consultation can also assist therapists in keeping their biases in check to avoid placing their values and opinion of normal development on their teen clients. It is additionally important for therapists to see an adolescent's developmental tasks not as distractions from therapy but instead as opportunities to support healthy and effective growth.

Independence vs. Support

INDEPENDENCE   BALANCE   SUPPORT

Independence. On this end of the dialectic, therapists are allowing autonomy and putting clients "in charge" of therapy. The pro of fostering autonomy in therapy is that it can increase investment in the process and assist teens in taking accountability for their participation and movement toward goals. However, remember that excessive independence can be a problem. Like parents, therapists need to avoid having adult expectations for teens (Miller, Rathus, Linehan, 2007). Therapists who allow for too much autonomy are at risk for a lack of therapeutic alliance and teamwork, leading to disengaged or unsupported teen clients. Additionally, therapists on this end of the dialectic may not provide enough structure or may have unclear rules or expectations, leading to overwhelmed or confused teen clients.

Offering Support. On this end of the dialectic, therapists offer support, guidance and problem solving. The advantage of this end of the dialectic is that teens have an active alliance with therapists and group. However, excessive support also becomes a problem. Excessive support can take a few different forms. For some, therapists become caretakers and are at risk for taking on their teen client's problems as their own. Therapists on this end of the extreme may be focused on being liked and accepted by their teen clients and may not have clear boundaries. This sets up an environment for enmeshment, which can only distract from learning skills and achieving therapeutic change. For others, therapists become too much of an advocate and solve problems for the teen, rather than encouraging him or her to address them independently (Miller, Rathus, Linehan, 2007). These therapists may have a rigid structure and expectations and not enough flexibility.

Balance. Remember that balance involves encouraging teenagers to take responsibility for elements of treatment *and* providing structure and support. Each teenager is different, and areas for support or independence will vary. Group skills training therapists need to be mindful of a balance that is most effective for each individual client and the group as a whole.

Therapists are encouraged to empower their teen clients to take ownership of as many aspects of treatment as possible. Encouraging independence within a framework of support can mean defaulting to the teen's decision making and problem solving. For most client concerns, give space and time for teens to create their own answers to their own struggles. Follow up by offering suggestions of ways to use DBT skills and facilitate group problem solving to bring forth each group client's ideas. For safety issues or therapy-interfering behaviors, therapists are encouraged to have a reliable structure for insuring safety and addressing behaviors that act as treatment barriers. Providing structure and solid expectations are needed in areas that are more serious or harmful, and these areas require less autonomy and more support.

There are many ways to offer support for areas that do not involve safety issues or therapy-interfering behaviors. Establish routine and treatment traditions so that clients know what to expect each session. Set and reinforce the group's rules and expectations consistently, and facilitate discussion on ways teens can hold each other accountable. Balance requires the therapist to use Wise Mind to recognize when space is productive and helpful and when support and stepping in is effective.

Being Strict vs. Lenient

STRICT	BALANCE	LENIENT

Strict. On this end of the dialectic, therapists provide clear structure, rules and expectations. Teen clients require structure, as it creates a stable and consistent therapy environment. However, problems are created when a therapist is too strict. Excessive rules and overly high expectations prevent teens from having the space they need to create and achieve their own therapy goals. Additionally, therapists who are too strict do not allow for the developmentally normative behaviors of adolescence. This creates an environment that is unsupportive of growth through the developmental stage of adolescence. Most importantly, therapists who are too strict sacrifice a strong therapeutic alliance with their teen clients. This prevents effective learning and actually brings the client and group further away from achieving DBT's treatment targets and functions.

Lenient. On this end of the dialectic, therapists provide plenty of room for clients to guide therapy. Teen clients also require this, as it allows them to practice their developmental task of increased autonomy. However, problems are also created when an emphasis is placed on being lenient. Not having structure, rules and expectations leads to inconsistency and a lack of therapeutic cohesion. Additionally, being too lenient with safety concerns and therapy-interfering behaviors is risky and acts as a significant barrier to change. Being too lenient leads to excessive distractions and a lack of focus on DBT's treatment targets and functions.

Balance. Balance with this dialectic requires the therapist to be mindful of DBT's treatment targets and functions. Therapists should work on DBT's treatment targets by having a structure for assessing and ensuring safety, addressing therapy and quality of life–interfering behaviors, and focus on skills training and generalization. Therapists should also be mindful of each individual client's motivation for change, as well as awareness of the group's attitude toward change.

Being mindful of DBT's treatment targets and functions will help the therapist recognize how strict or lenient to be with teen clients. The therapist's main role is to create structure and expectations that reinforce these treatment targets and functions. Then, therapists can focus on empowering teen clients to meet these expectations in their own way and guide them back to the targets when they stray too far.

Remember that safety concerns or therapy-interfering behaviors require less flexibility and are areas where the therapist needs to be stricter. Therapists can ease up on behaviors or treatment concerns that do not pose a threat to safety or therapy.

Parental Involvement vs. Therapeutic Privacy

PARENTAL INVOLVEMENT	BALANCE	THERAPEUTIC PRIVACY

Parental Involvement. Involving parents in a DBT program can increase support, skill use and communication at home. Additionally, parents who are involved in their teen's treatment can demonstrate less reactivity, as they have a greater understanding of their teen's mental health concerns. However, over-involvement of parents can become a barrier to effective DBT treatment. When parents are too involved, teens experience less trust and safety in the therapy environment. This may cause teens to be dishonest or not disclose topics they do not wish their parents to know. Additionally, treatment that overly involves parents reduces teens' autonomy and can diminish their ownership over their own goals and skill use.

Therapeutic Privacy. Having therapeutic privacy for teenagers can increase autonomy and motivation to independently work toward therapy goals. Therapeutic privacy can also enhance the client-therapist relationship and instill a sense of trust and safety in treatment. However, an over-focus on therapeutic privacy and not involving parents can also become a barrier to effective DBT treatment. When parents are not involved, communication and skill use as a family system is sacrificed. This leads to missed opportunities to address parent-teen problems and prevents parents from learning ways to support their teen in learning and using DBT at home. Additionally, too much therapeutic privacy prevents the parent from getting feedback about their contributions to concerns at home and further limits problem solving of these concerns. Parents who are disconnected from their teen's DBT treatment may have less tolerance for setbacks and lack recognition of a teen's work in therapy and progress made.

Balance. Balance on this dialectic means involving parents *and* having boundaries to ensure therapeutic privacy for the teenager. As discussed earlier, there are a variety of ways DBT programs incorporate parents. Whatever the method, therapists are encouraged to support teen clients' developmental task of autonomy when involving parents. Therapists can do so by asking teens to initiate and guide communication with parents. This at times requires coaching to assist the teen in identifying his or her goals for conversations with parents in therapy, as well as identification of ways to apply DBT skills to be effective in these conversations. Therapists are again encouraged to play a supporting role and to facilitate but not create the therapeutic process. If safety or other significant topics occur that the therapist feels the parents need to know, the therapist is encouraged to invite the teen to be involved in these conversations with parents. At times a teen will refuse, and the therapist will need to break therapeutic privacy to ensure safety. Although this is not the desired outcome, attempts for including the teen are generally appreciated and can minimize impacts to therapeutic trust. Balance on this dialectic can at times mean referrals for family therapy or individual therapy for a parent.

Create an Active Skills Group Environment

Learning activities are an effective and dynamic way to teach DBT skills to adolescents. Having an active group environment will promote learning and enhance engagement in the therapy (Miller, Rathus, Linehan, 2007). Following, we will explore the reasons for using activities, barriers to creating an active skills group environment and ways a therapist can promote hands-on learning. A Sample Documents section is provided in the last chapter of the therapist section of this book.

Benefits of Teaching DBT Skills With Activities

Recognizing the benefits of having an active group therapy environment will help you have an experiential attitude and approach. One functional reason for teaching with activities is that teenagers typically come to a DBT skills group after having been in school all day. This means they have been sitting in a classroom for 6 to 8 hours and are probably tired of listening to lectures. Having an experiential therapy environment can engage teenagers during a time of the day when they may want to disengage. Being active in a skills group is a way that teenagers can differentiate DBT from school (Miller, Rathus, Linehan, 2007).

Developmentally, teenagers are gaining new cognitive skills, and they have a greater understanding of abstract concepts. However, application of these abstract concepts is still novel, and teens may struggle to put some DBT skills into action. Practicing skills in therapy helps to bridge this gap and improves skill use. Teenagers are between childhood and adulthood, and an effective approach includes therapeutic techniques consistent with both child and adult therapy. In other words, lecture and discussion are still part of an effective DBT skills group for teens, but, like children, adolescents still like to play, and channeling energy into DBT activities also serves them well.

Activities, particularly team activities, help a group build cohesiveness and therapeutic alliance. Giving the group a common goal helps teenagers create strong working relationships. High levels of group cohesiveness can improve each teen's commitment to group and creates an atmosphere where both supportive and challenging feedback is given and accepted. Engaging with peers can improve a teen's confidence and provides positive experiences where he or she is part of a connected group of peers. Teaching with activities also helps teens meet their primary goal for joining a DBT group—learning, remembering and applying DBT skills.

Barriers to an Active Learning Environment

Like most things in therapy, creating an active environment comes with many barriers. Clients and therapists can create barriers to an active therapy environment. Awareness of these barriers will help you problem solve them as they occur.

Lack of group cohesion or of safety and trust in the group can be a significant barrier. If the group has not built relationships and established a level of security, getting teenage clients to engage in activities will be difficult. Group heterogeneity may be one factor that makes group cohesion more difficult. Clients may vary in age and developmental stage, socioeconomic status, gender, sexuality and religious or spiritual orientation. Your teenage clients may additionally present with a variety of mental health concerns.

Teenagers can be focused on how they are the same or different from others, and having significant differences with peers could lead to mistrust, difficulty communicating, cliques or variations in client disclosure. If this is the case, therapists may need to allow more time and focus on relationship building.

The mental health concerns with which teenagers come to therapy can also represent a barrier in creating an experiential environment. Developmentally, teenagers experience moodiness. This can be compounded by depression, anxiety or other mental health concerns. Teenagers in DBT often exhibit emotional dysregulation, which can result in refusal to participate, conflict with peers, attention-seeking behaviors or withdrawal and minimal participation. Emotional reactivity and crisis behaviors can present themselves and easily distract from learning activities. In addition, social anxiety is a common mental health concern, and teenagers who are socially phobic may be reluctant to participate in activities due to fear of rejection, judgment or embarrassment. Group peers who are interested and engaged in activities may get frustrated with a socially anxious teen who participates less. Distraction and difficulty concentrating can present as barriers to using activities. Teenagers can be easily distracted and can get off topic in an attempt to connect with group peers. It is developmentally typical for teens to have difficulty holding comments or observations about irrelevant topics. Alternatively, teen clients may have concentration and attention difficulties due to a mental health issue such as ADHD or anxiety. Or, teens may use distractions as a way to avoid difficult topics. Distractibility can be intensified with the excitement about an activity.

Therapists can also bring barriers to having an active environment. In comparison to lecture, using activities can feel like a risk. Therapists may feel insecure or have fears that the activity will be received poorly. Working with teenagers frequently requires working evening hours, and therapists at times work a full day before facilitating an evening DBT skills group. Therapists may avoid activities due to the extra planning and energy they require.

Creating an Active Environment: Therapist's Role

Therapists who facilitate an adolescent DBT skills group have a difficult task in establishing a group culture that is receptive to and effective with learning activities. A good place to start is by being comfortable with yourself in the moment (Miller, Rathus, Linehan, 2007). This requires you to be grounded in your own clinical orientation. Being comfortable with yourself as a therapist brings security to the group and allows you to easily recover if an activity "flops." Be present with your clients and allow the moment to unfold. Remember that you may not get the response you were expecting when trying an activity, but there still may be lessons in the response you get. Be honest and genuine in your interactions with your teen clients and remember that a sense of humor makes activities more enjoyable and engages your teens in learning. Balance your time at work with self-care activities outside of work. This can help you manage fatigue that may get in the way of being experiential in group.

Remember that safety and a cohesive group create an environment most conducive to hands-on learning. Establish a safe and cohesive group by modeling and reinforcing a Non-Judgmental Stance. Notice when your teen clients are using acceptance and validation and emphasize and reinforce this interaction. Immediately and consistently address judgmental or disrespectful feedback, which can appear as whispering, side conversations, eye rolling or negative feedback (Miller, Rathus, Linehan, 2007). Additionally, consistency and predictability will promote a safe and cohesive group. Teaching with activities can leave the impression that the regular group rules and structure do not apply. You can manage this by establishing a group structure when doing activities. For example, consider reviewing a skill before doing the activity that provides practice for it. After the activity, have a closing discussion about how the activity went. Creating this structure can help reign in expectations that doing an activity means being exempt from rules. Enforce group rules and provide supportive and positive feedback regularly. Being consistent and predictable also applies to your own mood and feedback. Be mindful of yourself before and during group and tend to stressors so you have a similar presentation each group session.

Activities for Teaching DBT

This section describes activities to teach DBT skills in each of the four DBT skill modules. The activities listed here can easily be applied in your adolescent DBT group, and most of them require few materials. Remember that there are many ways to teach DBT with group activities, and hopefully this section will not only provide you some concrete options but also spark your own creativity in developing new activities.

Each activity description includes the following:

- A unique activity name

- Supplies needed

- Preparation instructions (if they apply)

- Activity goal

- Activity instructions

- Discussion questions

The activity goal and discussion question are two essential components for using activities to teach DBT skills. Because it can be easy for both the teens and therapist to get sidetracked when doing an activity, the activity goal will help the therapist remain focused on the intent of the activity and can assist him or her in guiding the teens' attention to the purpose of the activity. Additionally, having a discussion after an activity is vital, and it is important that therapists factor in time for the discussion. It is through the discussion that teens are asked to think critically about their experience and how the experience applies to their daily life. This assists with skill generalization, a function of DBT.

Mindfulness Module

Mindfulness skills are central to everything in DBT. Mindfulness is crucial in helping teenagers slow down to make more planned decisions. Mindfulness helps teenagers increase awareness of emotions, thoughts, urges and body sensations. It is with this self-awareness that teenagers are able to apply DBT skills to make effective decisions and change troublesome patterns.

Unfortunately, Mindfulness skills are fairly abstract and require a lot of practice. For this reason, therapists are encouraged to frequently facilitate Mindfulness exercises and activities. Mindfulness activities are most effective when they include a thorough discussion of the Mindful experience. This allows teens to really recognize and engage with their internal reactions to external events. With all Mindfulness activities, remember that the goal is to help teenagers increase an understanding of themselves, their environment and the interplay between the two.

Observe, Describe & Participate

Activity name: Mystery Bags

Supplies needed:

- 3 or 4 medium-sized lunch or gift bags (works best when bags have handles)

- 3 or 4 items with a variety of textures (e.g., small stuffed animal, sugar, coffee beans)

Preparation instructions: Prepare the bags outside of group by putting one item in each bag.

Activity goal: Teach Observe, Describe & Participate in learning about self and environment.

Activity instructions:

- Note that group members will take turns reaching into each bag to Observe and Describe using only the sense of touch. Instruct group members to notice external events (the facts; e.g., rough, smooth, soft, hard) to Describe the item and internal experiences (such as judgments; e.g., gross, nice) about the item, body sensations, emotions and urges.

- Ask group members to especially notice urges, such as the urge to pull their hand away. Ask group members to Observe and Describe an urge and to Participate by not acting on the urge. Instruct group members to be gentle and Non-Judgmental if they do act on the urge. Remind group members that they can try again next time.

- Choose a bag to start with, and go around the room asking each group member one at a time to touch what is in the bag without looking. Ask that group members hold their observations until everyone has tried that bag.

- When each group member has had the opportunity to feel the item in the bag, have a short discussion by asking the following questions:

  What did the item feel like? Share just the facts.
  What judgments did you have when feeling the item?
  What other internal experiences did you notice? (Ask about body sensations, emotions, urges.)
  Were you able to surf the urge to pull away? What was it like to try?
  Did you notice any other urges? Did you act on them or surf the urge?
  What did you notice when other people put their hand in the bag? What was it like to observe others?

- Choose a second bag and again go around the room, giving each group member a chance to feel. Ask the same questions for each item.

Discussion questions:

- What was it like to use Observe and Describe? What did you learn about yourself or your environment?

- What was it like to Participate by not acting on urges?

- How could you use Observe, Describe and Participate in your day-to-day life?

- How do you think this could be helpful?

- What could help you to use Observe, Describe and Participate?

Activity

One-Mindfully

Activity name: Multi-Task Mixer

Supplies needed:

- Two games or tasks that require concentration (e.g., puzzle games, trivia questions, list of words to memorize, script for a text message)

- A timer if not included in game or task chosen.

Activity goal: Emphasize how One-Mindfully is more effective than multi-tasking.

Activity instructions:

- Ask for two volunteers to demonstrate One-Mindfully.

- Introduce the two games or tasks. Explain that volunteer #1 will practice multi-tasking by playing two games at once, and volunteer #2 will keep track of scores on the two games.

- Set a timer (not needed if playing a game with built-in timer) for 2 minutes.

- Volunteer #1 works on the two tasks simultaneously until the timer sounds (e.g., volunteer could be asked to send a lengthy text from a script you provide while also hearing and trying to memorize and repeat a list of words).

- After timer sounds, volunteer #2 writes down volunteer #1's score on the two games or tasks (e.g., 1 point for each word accurately written in text, number of correct words memorized)

- Next, volunteer #1 is asked to practice One-Mindfully by playing each game or task one at a time. Timer is again set for 2 minutes (unless game includes built-in timer).

- After timer sounds, volunteer #2 again writes down the scores for the two games or tasks.

Discussion questions:

- What did you notice about the scores when volunteer #1 was multi-tasking versus being One-Mindful?

- To volunteer #1: How did you feel when you were multi-tasking? How did you feel when you were One-Mindful?

- How often do you multi-task? How so?

- What gets in the way of being One-Mindful?

- What might help you practice the One-Mindful skill?

Non-Judgmental Stance

Activity name: Face the Facts

Supplies needed:

- 6 to 8 pictures of faces (can get pictures from magazines or print images from the internet)

- Small to medium mirrors (1 for each group member)

Preparation instructions: Cut out pictures of faces and paste or tape them on notecards.

Activity goal: Demonstrate how a Non-Judgmental Stance can improve acceptance and decrease difficult emotions.

Activity instructions:

- Each group member receives a notecard. Ask members not to show their picture to others.

- Explain that group members will use a Non-Judgmental Stance by describing the face on the notecard with only external information—no opinions or judgments.

- Ask for a volunteer to start by describing the face on his or her notecard using only facts (cannot say – "this person has pretty eyes," can say "this person's eyes are blue.")

- After group member finishes describing the face, he or she can show the group the note card.

- When each person has had a turn, hand out mirrors to each group member.

- Note that this time each group member will have the opportunity to describe his or her own face with a Non-Judgmental Stance.

- Instruct group members to look at their face in the mirror and describe it using only the facts. This description can be done out loud to whole group or each group member can Observe and Describe silently.

Discussion Questions:

- What was it like to use only the facts in describing faces in the pictures?

- What judgment words did you notice coming up?

- What did it feel like to focus on the facts?

- How might these feelings be different if you were using judgments?

- Were you able to picture the faces on the notecards with their descriptions?

- What was it like to use only the facts in describing your own face?

- What judgment words did you notice coming up?

- What did it feel like to focus on the facts?

- How might these feelings be different if you were using judgments?

- How could a Non-Judgmental Stance be helpful to you in your daily life?

- What might get in the way of using a Non-Judgmental Stance in your daily life?

Note: During the discussion, group members may express feeling that judgments would be helpful with descriptions. Validate this point, and remind group members that Non-Judgmental Stance does not mean *never* using judgments. Instead, the goal is to judge mindfully. Remind group members not to judge having judgments.

Distress Tolerance Module

The goal in using activities to teach the Distress Tolerance skills is to help teenage clients practice skills to manage stressors in the short term and to adopt a mindset that changes their relationship to stressors in the long term. An ongoing focus in the Distress Tolerance module is finding balance between approaching and avoiding stressors. This is particularly true when teaching the Crisis Survival skills.

Remember that Crisis Survival requires balance between dealing with the crisis and taking a break.

Breaks are meant to be temporary and planned. This means it is important to mindfully take a break.

Remember that avoiding a crisis leads to greater problems in the long term, and that dealing with a crisis is a necessary part of distress tolerance.

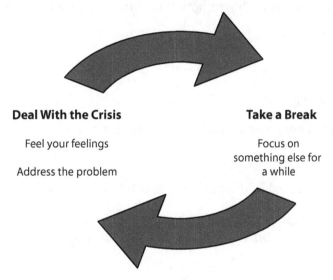

Deal With the Crisis

Feel your feelings

Address the problem

Take a Break

Focus on
something else for
a while

Assist clients in identifying when it is effective to manage stressors and when it is effective to take a break from stressors. Activities for the Wise Mind ACCEPTS, Self-Soothe, IMPROVE the Moment and Creative Outlet skills are included to teach effective ways to tolerate immediate stressors without making a difficult situation worse.

Wise Mind ACCEPTS

Each letter in ACCEPTS stands for a way to skillfully distract from a crisis or stressor. The activity goal and general instructions apply to the skill as a whole. An activity for each letter in ACCEPTS is provided, followed by discussion questions that apply to each activity in the skill.

Activity goal: Illustrate how Wise Mind ACCEPTS is about temporarily distracting from a crisis or stressor.

General instructions: Instruct group members to notice and rate their level of depression, anxiety or stress before and after the activity to highlight how Wise Mind ACCEPTS can be used to reduce focus on stressors and emotions.

A—Activities

Activity name: Board Game Day

Supplies needed: A favorite board game that all group members can play

Activity instructions:

- Remind clients that the goal of distracting with activities is to focus away from stressors.

- Ask clients to use activities as distraction by playing a board game together. Note that the goal is to focus away from stressors by engaging in the board game.

C—Contributing

Activity name: Create a Card

Supplies needed:

- Construction paper

- Markers, crayons

- Other art supplies as desired

Activity instructions:

- Note that in this activity, the group will practice Contributing by making a card for someone they care about.

- Ask group members to focus on caring feelings while making the card.

- While group members are working, facilitate discussion about who the card is being made for and why this person was chosen.

• Ask group members to use a Non-Judgmental Stance and Turn the Mind if they notice judgments about their card, and ask group members to focus on how it feels to Contribute.

C—Comparisons

Activity name: TV Comparisons

Supplies needed: Computer, IPad® or other medium to show video clips

Preparation instructions: Search the Internet for clips of difficult events from a dramatic teen TV show or movie. Examples include *Glee* or *Gossip Girl*. Look for a clip in which the characters are experiencing difficulties that group members are likely not facing. Remember to look for clips that are not triggering.

Activity instructions:

• Set up a computer, IPad or other medium to show video clip.

• Inform group members that they will practice the Comparisons skill by comparing their situation to that of the characters in the clip.

• After clip, facilitate a discussion about ways in which the group members are doing better than the characters in the clip.

E—Emotions

Activity name: Distract with Humor

Supplies needed: Computer, IPad or other medium to show video clips

Preparation instructions: Search the Internet for short and funny video clips. These could include clips of cats or dogs, scenes from funny movies or bloopers. YouTube.com is a popular site for funny clips. It is also recommended that clips are bookmarked for easy access.

Activity instructions:

• Set up a computer, IPad or other medium to show video clips.

• Show clips and ask group members to be mindful of their emotions and thoughts while watching them.

• Ask group members if they have clips they would like to share. Set desired parameters, such as no cursing in video or no clips that glamorize drinking or drug use.

P—Push Away

Activity name: Worry Box

Supplies needed:

• Shoebox sealed and decorated

• Notecards

Preparation instructions:

- Take a shoebox and tape it shut. Cut a slot in the top and decorate the box as desired.

Activity instructions:

- Ask group members to write down their worries or stressors on the notecards. Instruct group members to use as much detail as they need.

- Instruct group members to put their notecards into the box, and tell them that by doing so, they are making a choice to take focus away from their worries or stressors.

T—Thoughts

Activity name: Alphabet Animals

Supplies needed: None

Instructions:

- Explain that with this activity, group members will be asked to think of a type of animal that starts with each letter of the alphabet.

- Ask for a volunteer to start. He or she will start by naming an animal that begins with the letter A, such as *antelope*. The group member to his or her right with continue with the letter B, and so on. Ask participants to name their animal as quickly as possible.

Variations: Name all the items in the room that are blue, or have each group member say a word that is an increasing number of letters long (e.g., one letter = *a*, two letters = *of*, three letters = *the*).

S—Sensations

Activity name: That's Sense-Sational!

Supplies needed: A strong-tasting candy (e.g., cinnamon candy, sour candies, minty gum)

Instructions:

- Explain that group members will practice Sensations by eating something with a strong flavor.

- Hand out the chosen candy, and instruct group members to be mindful by focusing on its flavor.

Variations: Evoke a different sense. Examples include smelling potent scents, such as perfume, body spray or essential oils, or engaging the sense of touch by holding an ice cube or rubbing a smooth or rough rock.

ACCEPTS Discussion questions:

- What did you notice about your thoughts while you were using ACCEPTS?

- What did you notice about your emotions and urges while using ACCEPTS?

- When do you need to be distracted?

- How can you use this skill at home?

Self-Soothe

Activity name: Self-Soothe Kit

Supplies needed:

- One shoebox for each group member (can ask members to bring in a shoebox)

- Construction paper

- Markers and crayons

- Other desired art supplies (e.g., glitter, foam letters)

- Starter items for kits (e.g., trial-size lotions, lip gloss, squeeze balls)

Activity goal: Highlight the many ways that Self-Soothe can be used and the importance of having needed items available.

Activity instructions:

- Inform group members that a Self-Soothe kit will help them be prepared to use Self-Soothe when they need it.

- Hand out a shoebox to each group member.

- Instruct group members to decorate the box as they desire.

- Offer starter items for each kit and facilitate a conversation about other items that could be placed in the box.

- Ask group members to store their Self-Soothe kit in a place they are likely to see and remember it.

Discussion questions:

- What was it like to make a Self-Soothe kit?

- How will you know when you need the kit?

- Where will you put your Self-Soothe kit?

Activity

IMPROVE the Moment

Activity Goal: Highlight how IMPROVE the Moment can be used to make difficult events more positive.

I—Imagery

Activity name: My Happy Place Collage

Supplies needed:

- Construction paper

- 8 to 10 magazines that can be cut up

- Several pairs of scissors

- Glue or glue sticks

- Other desired art supplies

Activity instructions:

- Review how Imagery means using your imagination to create a more pleasant environment.

- Instruct group members to look through magazines and cut out pictures that represent a place that is happy and pleasant.

- Ask group members to create a collage with their pictures.

- Facilitate discussion during the activity about elements that would make for a safe and happy place. Encourage group members to post their collage someplace where they will need a reminder of Imagery.

M—Meaning

Activity name: Silver Linings List

Supplies needed:

- Paper

- Markers or colored pencils

Activity instructions:

- Remind group members that the Meaning skill is about focusing on the purpose, reason or positive parts of a difficult situations.

- Note that group members will work on Meaning together by making a Silver Linings List.

- Ask group members to think about good things that have come from difficult situations. Provide examples, such as "Depression helps me relate to other people better," or "I learned that I am a strong person because I got though something difficult."

- Each group member can make his or her own Silver Linings List or the group can make one list together.

P—Prayer

Activity name: My Prayer Options

Supplies needed:

- Envelopes or small boxes

- Notecards

- Markers or crayons

- Other are supplies as desired

Activity instructions:

- Remind group members that the Prayer skill can look different for different people. Note that today's activity will be about each group member using Prayer in his or her own way.

- Hand out envelopes or small boxes and several notecards to each group member.

- Ask group members to decorate their envelope or small box as they wish.

- Instruct group members to write on their notecards ways that they can Pray. Examples include meditation, take a walk, go to church, light a candle or create a prayer.

- When they have finished writing, ask group members to put their notecards in their envelope or box. Note that when they feel the desire or need to Pray, they can pull out a notecard for a reminder of how to use Prayer.

- Ask group members to put the envelope or box someplace they will need it, such as in their room, backpack or locker at school.

R—Relaxation

Activity name: Spa DBT

Supplies needed:

- Relaxing music

- Tea or hot chocolate

- Soothing lotion

- Pillows or soft throw blankets

Activity instructions:

- Remind group members that Relaxation is about helping your body and mind feel calmer. Note that Relaxation can be different for everyone, and group members will be asked to practice a few common Relaxation activities.

- Ask group members to choose a pillow or throw blanket and get comfortable in their seat or on the floor.

- Ask for a volunteer to serve tea or hot chocolate to other group members.

- Play relaxing music, such as instrumental or classical music.

- Offer soothing lotion to interested group members.

- Facilitate a deep breathing exercise.

- Instruct clients to be mindful of each activity and focus on what it feels like to Relax.

- Facilitate discussion about the Relaxing nature of the activities and what additional activities group members could try at home.

O—One Thing at a Time

Activity name: One Piece at a Time

Supplies needed: Jenga® game

Activity instructions:

- Remind group members that the One Thing at a Time skill helps to IMPROVE the Moment by focusing on only one step at a time.

- Set up the game Jenga® and ask clients to play by only focusing on one piece at a time.

- Facilitate discussion about how focusing on more than one piece at a time can be overwhelming and ineffective, as the player will not know what the stack of blocks will look like after the next player takes a turn. Discuss how focusing on one piece at a time will help the player be focused and Effective in the moment.

V—Vacation

Activity name: Let's Take a Trip

Supplies needed: Supplies needed will depend on vacation chosen.

Activity instructions:

- The session before the activity, teach group members that the goal of the Vacation skill is to IMPROVE the Moment by doing something special and temporarily leaving stressors behind. Note that at the next session, the group will be practicing the Vacation skill by creating a Vacation spot in group.

• Facilitate a group discussion about possible "destinations," such as Hawaii or Paris. Discuss ways the group could bring this Vacation to life in group, such as making paper leis or learning French phrases. Identify ways the group can work together to bring the Vacation to life next group.

• In preparation for the Vacation group, gather needed items. Consider putting up simple decorations in the group room.

• At the start of group, remind members that their goal is to focus on their Vacation spot and to enjoy themselves. Note that this requires temporarily leaving their stressors behind.

• As the activity time comes to an end, ask group members to recap their experience and remind them they can recall their positive memories as a way to IMPROVE the Moment. Note that the Vacation skill is meant to be a temporary break, and when the Vacation is over, direct group members back to group tasks.

E—Encouragement

Activity name: You Can Do It! I Can Do It!

Supplies needed:

• Paper

• Markers or crayons

Activity instructions:

• Explain that group members will be asked to practice Encouragement with this activity. Note that often it is easier to encourage others than it is to encourage ourselves.

• Ask group members to write their name on the top of the paper. Note that group members can make their name as decorative as they want.

• Once each group member has a sheet of paper with his or her name on the top, ask group members to pass their paper to the person on their right.

• Instruct group members to write something Encouraging on their peer's paper. Note that it should be a statement that their peer would need to hear during a difficult time.

• Continue to pass the papers to the right, with each group peer writing an Encouraging statement on each paper, until each paper returns to the person whose name is on top.

• Ask clients to keep their paper when they are likely to need Encouragement (such as in a locker at school or on the mirror in the bathroom). Note that the statements on the paper were written by someone else but can also be used by ourselves as Encouragement when we need it.

IMPROVE the moment Discussion questions:

• What did you notice about your thoughts when practicing IMPROVE the Moment?

• What did you notice about your emotions or urges when practicing IMPROVE the Moment?

• How could you use this skill outside of group?

• What might help you be prepared to use IMPROVE the Moment when you need it?

Activity

Creative Outlet

Activity name: My Artistic Expression

Supplies needed:

- Construction paper

- Markers, crayons

- Other art supplies as desired

Activity goal: Highlight how the Creative Outlet skill can help to skillfully release emotional energy.

Activity instructions:

- Remind group members that the Creative Outlet skill is about releasing emotional energy by getting in touch with your creative side.

- Ask group members to try the Creative Outlet skill by making an art project of their own. Note that they can write, draw, color or complete other art projects.

- Remind group members to use their Non-Judgmental Stance and focus on expressing themselves.

Discussion questions:

- What was it like to use the Creative Outlet skill?

- Did you notice judgments coming up? If so, were you able to use a Non-Judgmental Stance?

- How did it feel to use the Creative Outlet skill? Did your emotions change during or after using the Creative Outlet skill?

- How could you use this skill in your daily life?

Activity

Turn the Mind

Activity name: It's All a Matter of Perspective

Supplies needed: An object that looks different from a variety of angles (e.g., a teddy bear, a sculpture)

Activity goal: Teach that there are many ways to see the same thing and that people can make a choice to Turn the Mind to focus on a perspective that improves acceptance.

Activity instructions:

- Explain that the Turn the Mind skill is about finding a new way to look at the same situation so that you can move toward Radical Acceptance.

- Note that this activity will help group members see how there are many ways to look at the same thing.

- Place object on a table in the middle of the room and ask group members to sit in a circle around the item.

- Instruct group members to take a moment to Observe the item. Ask for a volunteer to start by Describing what he or she Observed by sharing just the facts. The group member to the volunteer's right is then asked to Describe his or her Observations. Continue this way until everyone has had the opportunity to share his or her view of the object.

- Facilitate discussion about the different descriptions of the object. Note that everyone was looking at the same thing, but each person had his or her own unique view of the item.

Discussion questions:

- What did you notice about the group's description of the item?

- How do you think you could use Turn the Mind in your day-to-day life?

- In what situations do you think you need Turn the Mind most?

Emotion Regulation Module

The Emotion Regulation module assists clients in building a more effective relationship with their emotions.

Activities in this module are at times used to evoke emotions so that clients can improve in their ability to identify, experience and express emotions (Miller, Rathus, Linehan, 2007). The activities used in the Emotion Regulation module can be paired with the Distress Tolerance activities to bring up difficult emotions followed by taking a break with Crisis Survival skills to manage triggered emotions.

Emotions - The Big Picture

Activity name: Interpretations

Supplies needed: Event Cards (see next page)

Activity goal: Illuminate how our thoughts about events can have a big impact on how we feel and how we act.

Activity instructions:

- Review the worksheet "Emotions: The Big Picture" (p. 63) and discuss how our interpretations of events have a big impact on how we end up feeling and acting.

- Ask for a volunteer to start the game. Note that the goal of the game is for the group to identify as many possible interpretations to the same event as possible.

- Instruct the volunteer to pick out an Event Card and make an interpretation of the event. Example: (In response to the event of calling a friend who does not answer) "My friend hates me and never wants to talk to me again."

- Instruct group members to go around the room and share another interpretation for the same event. (Example: Next client may say, "My friend didn't answer because she is in the shower.")

- Once all the interpretations are made, the next group member picks an Event Card and again goes around until the group cannot think of any more interpretations for the event.

Discussion questions:

- What do you think about how many interpretations the group was able to find for each event?

- Pick out certain interpretations and ask yourself how you might feel if that is the way you saw the situation. How might you act if you saw the situation that way?

- What skills do you think you could use to help with the way you interpret a situation?

    How could you use Radical Acceptance or Turn the Mind to help with how you see situations?

    How could Observe and Describe help?

    How could you use a Non-Judgmental Stance to manage your interpretations?

Event Cards

You texted your friend an hour ago, and she still hasn't sent a text back.

Your significant other cancels the date you have planned this weekend.

A peer looks like he or she is winking at you on the bus.

You see some classmates at the end of the hall whispering and looking in your direction.

Your mom is 20 minutes late picking you up from school.

Your teacher asks you to stay after class.

Observe & Describe Emotions

Activity name: Feelings Ball

Supplies needed:

- Small soccer ball or a ball with several different edges or sides

- Sharpie® marker

Activity goal: Increase recognition and understanding of emotions.

Preparation instructions:

- Write feeling words on each edge or side of ball. (It is recommended that the ball include feeling words that represent a range of the same emotion, such as annoyed, angry, enraged.)

- Write the following questions on a whiteboard or paper so all group members can see:

    Share a time you experienced this emotion.
    What do you notice about your body or thoughts when you experience this emotion?
    When was the last time you had this emotion?
    What is it like when someone around you experiences this emotion?

Activity instructions:

- Inform the group that today they will practice using Observe and Describe with emotions.

- Ask for a volunteer to start, and toss the ball to that person. Once he or she has caught the ball, ask him or her to read the emotion that appears on the ball under his or her pointer finger. Reference the list of questions and pick one to ask the volunteer about the emotion.

- Once that person has shared, he or she then tosses the ball to another group member, who again reads the emotion that appears under his or her pointer finger. The member who threw the ball now gets to ask a question of the person who caught the ball.

- Continue to have the group toss the ball until everyone has had at least one chance to Observe and Describe an emotion.

Discussion questions:

- What was it like to Observe and Describe emotions?

- Did you notice feeling comfortable or uncomfortable in talking about certain emotions?

- How do you think Observing and Describing emotions could be helpful in your daily life?

Activity

PLEASE

Activity name: Healthy Eating Socialization

Supplies needed: A variety of foods

Activity goal: Highlight ways to practice balanced eating.

Activity instructions: Have a social hour enjoying a variety of fruits, vegetables, nuts and sweets.

Discussion questions:

- What foods did you like or not like?

- What was it like to practice balanced eating together?

- What does it mean to have balanced eating?

- How can you improve your balanced eating?

- How could a Non-Judgmental Stance help with improving your eating habits?

Activity

Build Mastery

Activity name: Goal Getters!

Supplies needed:

- "Build Mastery: Group Goals" chart (see next page)

- Stickers

Activity goal: Illuminate how goal setting can Build Mastery.

Activity instructions:

- Note that together the group will Build Mastery by setting and working on a group goal. Facilitate discussion about areas in which the group can improve. Examples include timeliness to group, giving each other challenging feedback and staying focused during DBT teaching. If the group cannot identify an area in which to improve, facilitate discussion about new skills the group could work on building together. Examples include practicing mindfulness or increasing assertiveness.

- Assist the group in identifying small steps and ways to hold each other accountable in accomplishing the goal, as well as a reward for their work. Assist the group in making the goal objective and measurable.

- Fill in the "Build Mastery: Group Goals" chart to track progress on the goals. Stickers can be given for each day that the goal is accomplished.

Discussion questions:

- Do you think our group goal is reasonable? Achievable?

- What was it like to work together to set a goal?

- Why is it helpful to break a goal into small steps?

- How can you use goal setting to Build Mastery outside of group?

Build Mastery: Group Goals

Group Goal: _____

Small Step: _____ Target: _____ _____ times/week

Date: _____	Date: _____	Date: _____	Date: _____
Date: _____	Date: _____	Date: _____	Date: _____
Date: _____	Date: _____	Date: _____	Date: _____
Date: _____	Date: _____	Date: _____	Date: _____

Feel Your Feelings

Activity name: How Does That Make You Feel?

Supplies needed:

- Computer, IPad or other device set up with video clips

- Music player

Activity goal: Help group members identify and experience their emotions.

Preparation instructions:

- Find one or two emotional video clips. A clip from the movie *Up*, called "Carl and Ellie Through the Years" is recommended and can be found on YouTube.com.

- Identify an emotional song to share with group.

Activity instructions:

- Review the worksheet "The Big Picture of Emotions" (p. 53). Discuss how emotions change our body sensations, action urges and communication.

- Explain that members are going to see or hear YouTube clips and/or songs. Instruct members to feel their feelings when watching or listening.

- Play clip or song and follow up with discussion.

Discussion questions:

- What emotions did you notice coming up?

- How do you know you were feeling that way?

- How did your body feel?

- Did you have urges?

- Did your facial or body expressions change?

- What is it like to have this emotion?

Interpersonal Effectiveness Module

Practice is essential in learning and living the Interpersonal Effectiveness skills. Role-plays are one of the main vehicles for practice in a skill group setting. Although this is an effective way to learn and use the Interpersonal Effectiveness skills, teen clients can experience anxiety about role-playing, especially involving topics that hit close to home. Role-plays are more comfortable when seriousness is balanced by silliness, and it is recommended that introductory role-plays be lighthearted. Therapists are also encouraged to be active participants in the role-plays and to reinforce participation (Miller, Rathus, Linehan, 2007).

Because role-plays are an effective teaching tool, the majority of activities listed for the Interpersonal Effectiveness skills are examples of teen-specific scenarios to act out. Therapists are also encouraged to use the worksheets from the Interpersonal Effectiveness module in Part One to help teen clients identify real-life situations to practice in group. Therapists are also encouraged to frequently reference "My Relationships Evaluation" on pages 75 to 78 throughout the Interpersonal Effectiveness module. This will help teens improve their understanding of how skills practiced in group can be brought to life in their relationships outside of group.

Therapists are also reminded to seize opportunities for teen clients to practice the Interpersonal Effectiveness skills in their relationships with each other. Conflict in group is bound to happen, and therapists can assist their clients in using Interpersonal Effectiveness skills to settle the conflict and practice mending relationships after a conflict. In addition, a skills group is an excellent setting for teens to build effective working relationships with peers in whom they may not be interested as friends.

Types of Communication

Activity name: How Unskillful Can You Be?

Supplies needed:

- Scenario Cards (see next page)

- Unskillful Communication Cards (see next page)

- Optional—costumes or clothes to play "dress up"

Activity goal: Illuminate what unskillful forms of communication look like and how Interpersonal Effectiveness skills are a more effective way to communicate.

Activity instructions:

- Prior to teaching the Interpersonal Effectiveness skills, discuss unskillful forms of communication, which include passive, aggressive and passive-aggressive. Teach examples of what these forms of communication look like and why they are unskillful.

- Note that today group members will get a chance to practice being unskillful.

- Ask group members to split up into three groups. Each sub-group will be assigned an unskillful form of communication.

- Hand out Scenario Cards (the scenario should be fairly simple; e.g., your friend asks you for a ride home from school).

- Give each sub-group 5 to 10 minutes to create a skit in which one of the group members acts very unskillfully, according to his or her assigned unskillful form of communication (e.g., group discusses how to play out the scenario with one group member being aggressive).

- Group members can dress up to get into role if they desire.

- Each sub-group then presents their skit to the group, demonstrating their unskillful form of communication.

Discussion questions:

- What did you notice about this form of communication?

- Why was it unskillful?

- Do you think the person acting unskillful will get what he or she wants? Why or why not?

- How do you think the people around the unskillful person felt?

- How do you think the unskillful person felt about him- or herself?

- What do you think the long-term impact of this type of communication might be?

Unskillful Communication Cards

Passive

Aggressive

Passive-Aggressive

Scenario Cards

Your friend asks for a ride home from school almost every day.

You want to borrow your mom's car to take your friends to a concert this weekend.

Your peers have side conversations in class, and this makes it hard to focus.

GIVE

Activity name: Our Give Chart

Supplies needed:

- Give Chart (see next page)

- Star Stickers

Activity goal: Highlight how GIVE creates healthy and connected relationships.

Activity instructions:

- Discuss how this activity will be ongoing and will be used to help group members notice how they use GIVE with each other.

- Facilitate discussion about what it looks like to use the GIVE skill and why GIVE is important in group.

- Post the GIVE Chart in the group room and provide stickers. Begin the activity by identifying how a group member uses GIVE, and post a sticker next to his or her name on the chart. Encourage group members to catch each other using GIVE and when they do, put a sticker next to their name.

Discussion questions:

- How did it feel to use the GIVE skill?

- How did it feel to be the recipient of GIVE?

- How do you think GIVE impacted your relationship with your peer?

- How could you use GIVE in your day-to-day life?

- What relationships do you think especially need GIVE?

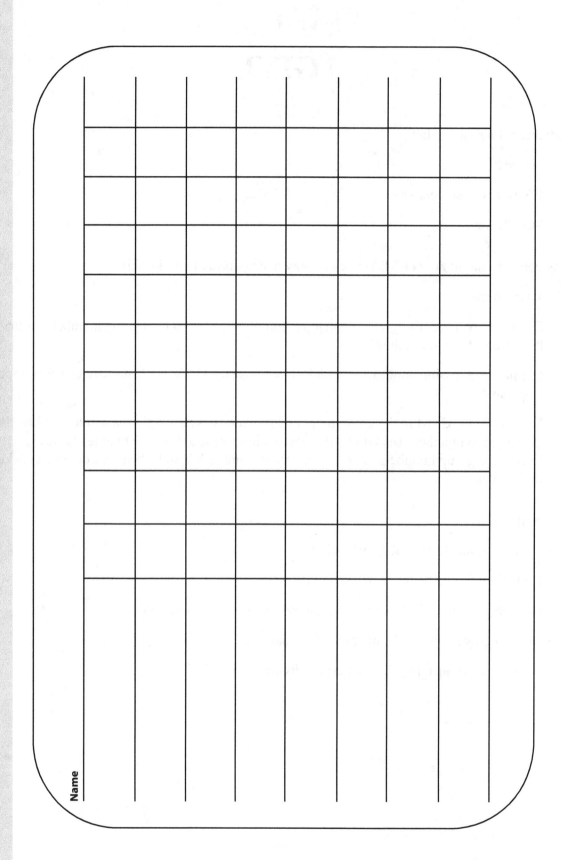

Our GIVE Chart

Name

Validation

Activity name: Validation Role-Plays

Supplies needed: Validation Scenarios List (see next page)

Activity goal: Highlight how Validation increases understanding and builds connections with others.

Activity instructions:

- Ask for a volunteer to begin the role-plays. Volunteer chooses a scenario from the Validation Scenarios List and (if needed) is instructed to ask the group for a second volunteer for help in acting out the scenario.

- Volunteer #1 reads the scenario to the group, and volunteer #2 begins the scenario by playing the part of person needing Validation. Volunteer #1 then practices giving only Validating feedback to volunteer #2.

- Continue until each group member has had the opportunity to practice giving Validation.

Discussion questions:

- What was it like to use Validation?

- What was it like to receive Validation?

- What made it difficult to Validate?

- What was it like to use Validation when you disagreed or were fighting?

- How could you use Validation in your relationships?

- How could you Validate yourself?

Validation Scenarios List

1. You are at lunch with several friends. You notice that one has been very quiet, avoids eye contact and looks like she is tearing up. Use Validation with her.

2. You are having a hard day and find it difficult to get homework done. To make matters worse, you keep calling yourself "stupid and lazy." Use Validation with yourself.

3. You really want to go to a party with your best friend, but, he says, "I don't think I'm in the mood for a party." Use Validation with your best friend.

4. A peer in your DBT skills group says she is really depressed. Use Validation with your group peer.

5. You and your mom are arguing about what time curfew should be. Use Validation with your mom.

6. Your dad is upset about losing his wallet and keys. Use Validation with him.

7. Your friend tells you at lunch that he got an A on his biology test. Use Validation with him.

8. Your brother tells you that he is thinking about breaking up with his girlfriend, and feels both sad and excited about it. Use Validation with your brother.

9. You studied really hard for a math test but ended up getting a C when you thought you'd get an A or a B. Use Validation with yourself.

10. Your mom just found out about your self-injury and is telling you how scared she is for your future. Use Validation to express an understanding of her perspective.

11. You and your friend are hanging out and want to get lunch, but you disagree about where to eat. Use Validation to express an understanding of your friend's opinion.

Activity

DEAR MAN

Activity name: DEAR MAN Role-Plays

Supplies needed: DEAR MAN Scenarios List (see next page)

Activity goal: Highlight how DEAR MAN creates effective relationships by making requests and saying no.

Activity instructions:

- Ask for a volunteer to begin the role-plays. Volunteer chooses a scenario from the DEAR MAN Scenarios List and is instructed to ask the group for a second volunteer for help in acting it out.

- Volunteer #1 reads the scenario to the group, and volunteer #2 begins the scenario by playing the part of person receiving the request. Volunteer #1 then practices a DEAR MAN with volunteer #2.

- Continue until each group member has had the opportunity to practice DEAR MAN.

Discussion questions:

- What was it like to use DEAR MAN?

- What did you think you did well in DEAR MAN?

- What areas of DEAR MAN do you think you could do differently?

- What was it like to receive DEAR MAN?

- What made it difficult to use DEAR MAN?

- How could you use DEAR MAN in your relationships?

DEAR MAN Scenarios List

1. You want to go out to a movie with friends tomorrow night. Your mom thinks you should stay home and catch up on homework instead. Use DEAR MAN to discuss this situation with her.

2. Your friend has been smoking in your car when you drive him to school. Use DEAR MAN to address this with him.

3. Your friend wants you to go to a concert with her, but you really don't like the band and don't want to spend the money on a ticket. Use DEAR MAN to say no to your friend's request.

4. Your friend has been calling you late at night, and it's been keeping you from getting enough sleep. Use DEAR MAN to address this with your friend.

5. Your best friend has been talking to you about his or her self-injurious behavior. This is very triggering for you, and you are finding it hard to control your own self-injurious behavior. Use DEAR MAN to set a limit with your best friend.

6. You are way behind on your homework and are having a hard time keeping up. Use DEAR MAN with your teacher to ask for an extension on the assignments.

7. You have a really big test coming up and need to study, but your friends keep emailing and texting, asking for you to go out with them. Use DEAR MAN to address this with your friends.

8. Your mom bad-mouths your dad when you get back from a weekend at your dad's. Use DEAR MAN to ask for limits with what she says about your dad.

9. Your mom says that you play too many video games and wants you to only play on the weekends. Use DEAR man with her to ask for what you want.

10. Your science teacher covers class material too fast, and you are having a difficult time keeping up in class. Use DEAR MAN with him or her to ask the teacher to go at a slower pace.

11. Your classmates are having a side conversation in your Social Studies class, and it's distracting you from the lesson. Use DEAR MAN to ask them to have their conversation during a break.

FAST

Activity name: FAST Role-Plays

Supplies needed: FAST Scenarios List (see next page)

Activity goal: Highlight how FAST improves self-respect in relationships.

Activity instructions:

- Ask for a volunteer to begin the role-plays. Volunteer chooses a scenario from the FAST Scenarios List and is instructed to ask the group for a second volunteer for help in acting out the scenario.

- Volunteer #1 reads the scenario to the group, and volunteer #2 begins the scenario by playing the part of person receiving the FAST skill. Volunteer #1 then practices FAST with volunteer #2.

- Continue until each group member has had the opportunity to practice FAST.

Discussion questions:

- What was it like to use FAST?

- What did you think you did well in FAST?

- What areas of FAST do you think you could do differently?

- Why do you think FAST is a self-respect skill? How did FAST impact the way you feel about yourself?

- What was it like to receive the FAST skill?

- What made it difficult to use FAST?

- How could you use FAST in your relationships?

FAST Scenarios List

1. You are shopping with your friend, who asks for your honest opinion about an outfit she tried on, which you dislike. Use FAST to be truthful with your friend.

2. You are at a party and some of your acquaintances ask if and your friend want to try marijuana. Your friend says yes, but doing drugs is against your values. Use FAST to handle the situation.

3. Your friend is upset because you said no when she asked you to go to a football game. Use your FAST skill to discuss the situation with her.

4. Your parents really want you to join an after-school club, but there aren't any that interest you. Use your FAST skill to discuss it with them.

5. Your mom wants to know if you are still using self-injury to cope with stress. Although you self-injured once last week, you are afraid to talk to your mom about it because she gets really upset when you tell her. Use your FAST skill to handle the situation.

6. Your partner drinks and you don't. Use FAST to deal with this when you are hanging out with friends and your partner wants to drink.

7. This Saturday, your parents want you to stay home, watch movies and play board games to get in some "good family time," but your friend is throwing a party and everyone will be there. Use FAST to discuss this with your parents.

8. You studied really hard and got an A on your geometry final. Your two best friends didn't study as hard and got bad grades. They want to know how you did on the final. Use FAST to respond to this situation.

9. Your basketball coach wants you to go to an extra practice to get ready for a big game, but the practice is scheduled at the same time that you have DBT. Use FAST to deal with this situation.

Values

Activity name: Values Collage

Supplies needed:

- Construction paper

- Magazines to cut up

- Several bottles of glue or glue sticks

- Several pairs of scissors

Activity goal: Reinforce how sticking to Values increases self-respect.

Activity instructions:

- Ask group members to review their Values.

- Explain that this activity is about creating a collage of pictures or words that are symbolic of their Values.

- While group members are working, facilitate conversation about what Values are and which Values are most important to each member. Discuss how the collage can be a reminder to Stick to values.

Discussion questions:

- What are your Values?

- How does it feel to think about and make a collage of your Values?

- Why do you think it's important to Stick to values?

- How could you remember and Stick to values in your daily life?

Sample Documents

This section includes example documents for working with teenagers in DBT. These documents can be used in a DBT skills group or individual therapy.

Following are descriptions of these documents and brief instruction for their use.

Commitment to DBT

Commitment agreements are important documents in a DBT program. The commitment agreement has several purposes. First, the thought and behavioral patterns addressed by DBT are serious, particularly when it comes to safety. Beginning therapy with a commitment sets a tone of seriousness, which these patterns deserve. Second, the items on the commitment agreement highlight DBT's treatment hierarchy and clearly lay out what will be focused on in the program (Miller, Rathus, Linehan, 2007). Last, coming to DBT is generally not a teenager's idea, as he or she is often encouraged or signed up by parents. A commitment agreement is a way therapists can talk with the teen about what he or she wants to get out of the program and make it clear that although the teen may not have signed up, it is ultimately his or her decision to make changes.

DBT Skills Group Rules and Expectations

Group rules and expectations are essential in facilitating a DBT skills group. By establishing clear boundaries, therapists are providing a structured and effective group experience. Therapists are encouraged to review DBT Skills Group Rules and Expectations regularly. If facilitating an open group, therapists are encouraged to review this document with the whole group each time a new group member joins. Therapists are additionally encouraged to facilitate discussion about why each rule exists.

An activity that has been helpful is putting each rule on a notecard, dealing the cards out so that each group member has at least one. Ask for a volunteer to start by reading the rule on his or her notecard. The person to the volunteer's right then explains the purpose of that rule. Other group members can add their thoughts on the rule, and when it has adequately been explained, the next rule is read and explained until all the rules have been discussed.

Encourage group cohesion and the development of autonomy by encouraging group members to hold each other accountable for following the group rules and expectations. This often begins with the therapist modeling assertiveness skills to address a group member who is breaking a rule and then encouraging discussion about how group members can do this themselves. At times this requires the therapist to give extra space and flexibility when a group rule or expectation is broken so that group members have time to feel discomfort and have space to figure out how to address broken group rules. The therapist's task here is to allow space while also ensuring the group does not become ineffective or unsafe. Encourage discussion of how the group can work together to maintain the rules and expectations and remember to notice and reinforce effectiveness in the moment.

My Crisis Survival Plan and My Safety Contract

The worksheets titled My Crisis Survival Plan and My Safety Contract are skills plans for teens to be prepared for crisis situations, particularly those involving safety concerns such as suicidal ideation (SI) and self-injurious behavior (SIB). Each teen is asked to create a skills plan when he or she begins DBT and to update it as he or she progresses through the program. Teens can complete these together or individually in group or outside of group as homework. If safety issues are reported in session, a skills plan should be in place before the client leaves for the day.

My Crisis Survival Plan is more detailed and specific and is used when a client is familiar with the Crisis Survival Skills in the Distress Tolerance module. Clients are asked to identify indicators that skills are needed and then are to identify several ways they can use each Crisis Survival Skill. My Safety Contract is less specific and open to DBT skills outside of the Crisis Survival Skills. My Safety Contract may be of particular help to teens who are just beginning DBT and are less familiar with the Distress Tolerance module. With each worksheet, teens are committing to follow their safety plan or call 911 if needed to maintain safety. It should also be noted that having teens list their group peers on their safety plan is discouraged. Teens in a skills group should not rely on each other for safety, as doing so puts too much pressure on the group peer and can trigger SI or SIB in the helper.

Adolescent DBT Diary Card

The goal of the Diary Card is to help the teenage client increase his or her mindfulness of symptoms, relationships, skills and stressors (Miller, Rathus, Linehan, 2007). In order to reinforce self-awareness and mindfulness of skills, clients are asked to complete a Diary Card each day. Daily compliance with the Diary Card can be a difficult feat for adolescent clients. Often you will hear, "I forgot about it," or "I didn't want to bring it to school." While it's easy to understand a teen's obstacles to completing a Diary Card daily, it is an essential piece of DBT. Work with your teens to identify and problem solve what gets in the way of doing a Diary Card each day. Consider making Diary Card completion a group goal and offer a reward (such as socialization time) when the group meets their goal.

The adolescent Diary Card is broken into sections, each with its own goal for daily tracking. As DBT is hierarchical, SI, SIB and therapy-interfering behavior (TIB) are the first items on the Diary Card. For these items, clients report the intensity of an urge on a scale of 0 to 10 (with 10 being the most intense), followed by a report of yes or no to indicate if these urges were acted on. Separating urge and action is of particular importance for teenage clients, who often struggle to postpone action when experiencing an urge. Separating urge and action with SI is also essential when doing safety assessments. Therapists need to know intensity of thoughts/urges and whether a client has progressed further with plans or has taken any steps toward acting on these thoughts/urges. Additionally, a common first step in working on SIB and TIB is being able to put distance between when a teen first feels an urge and when he or she acts on it. One way in which teens find success in stopping SIB is by first delaying action on urges, substituting action on SIB or TIB with a DBT skill. Over time, teens will experience success with DBT skills, with the final goal being replacement of SIB and TIB with DBT skills. This change takes time, and like any habit, takes a lot of practice and repetition. Tracking urges and action on a Diary Card can illuminate change over time.

In addition to SI, SIB and TIB, clients are asked to rate the intensity of three significant emotions: depression, anxiety and anger. Again, clients report these emotions on a scale of 0 to 10, with 10 being the most intense. At times, teenage clients will only intervene when their emotions are in the most intense range. Unfortunately, interventions can be more difficult to apply and can have a minimal impact when emotional intensity is high. Using a Diary Card to track levels of emotions can assist teenagers in recognizing lower levels of emotions, allowing them to more proactively apply DBT skills. This is also helpful practice in being able to notice and appreciate a wide variety of emotions and levels of intensity.

Teen clients are asked to be mindful of and track their use of the PLEASE skill on the Diary Card. The intention of daily mindfulness to the PLEASE skill is reducing emotional vulnerability and promoting an understanding that physical health contributes to mental health and vice versa. Clients are asked to track balanced exercise, balanced eating, balanced sleep, taking medication as prescribed and avoiding drugs and alcohol. Many teenagers struggle with body image and as a result engage in poor self-care. Tracking this on a Diary Card allows the therapist to seize opportunities for psychoeducation about balanced eating and exercise. Additionally, it is typical for teenagers to use drugs and alcohol, and use can vary with each client, including experimentation, abuse and addiction. Tracking use on a Diary Card can illustrate the extent of use to both the client and the therapist and allows for discussions about skills that could help to manage urges to use. Teen clients are asked to notice and track their DBT skill use each day. The DBT skills list can be used in adjunct to the Diary Card, and teens can use the skill abbreviations to make daily tracking easier.

Teen clients are also asked to be mindful of and rate the effectiveness of their relationships. This rating, again, occurs on a scale of 0 to 10, this time with 10 being excellent or highly effective. Relationships with friends, parents and other relatives are rated. Teen clients are also asked to rate their relationship with himself or herself. The goal with self-rating is placing emphasis on building a healthy self-concept and recognition of ways a teen can influence his or her opinion of himself or herself. This provides a balance to a teen's typical developmental behavior of over-focusing on relationships with others. An extension of this balance is tracking the use of Build Mastery and Build Positive Experiences. In each category, teen clients are encouraged to identify ways in which are actively creating emotional experiences of confidence and joy. The last category includes current and upcoming stressors paired with DBT skills that could be used to cope with these stressors. The goal is to assist teens in thinking ahead and identifying concrete ways they can apply skills to daily life stressors.

TIB Worksheet

Clients are asked to report on their TIB urges and actions every day, so it is important to spend some time clarifying what a TIB is. The TIB worksheet can be given to clients to complete individually, or the skills group facilitator could take teaching time to talk about TIB and complete the worksheet in group. Therapists are also encouraged to provide this handout to new clients so they can become familiar with the idea. The goal of the TIB worksheet is to help teens identify behaviors that are preventing them from being effective in DBT. Ask teens to think and talk about their TIB with a Non-Judgmental Stance to avoid undue guilt and shame and to focus on being effective in addressing their TIB.

DBT Skills List

The DBT Skills List is used with the Diary Card and acts as a key to the DBT skills. The skills list includes abbreviations for each skill so that teens can quickly and easily report on and communicate their skill use. The skills list also serves to help teens identify and remember the DBT skills and how they fit into each module.

Emotion Words

At times, teen clients will have difficult identifying their emotions or level of emotional intensity. The Emotion Words handout provides a starting place for these teens in identifying their own emotions. Having a variety of words for emotions can also assist teens in making sense of their own emotions and in expressing their feelings to others.

Behavior Chain

A Behavior Chain is an essential DBT tool and is particularly helpful for teenage clients. A Behavior Chain will help teens practice mindfulness to identify their internal reactions to events and link them to their behaviors and the outcome of their behaviors (Miller, Rathus, Linehan, 2007). Behavior Chains should be assigned when a teen acts on SIB or TIB, as these are treatment targets deserving of awareness and problem solving. Behavior Chains can also be used for other problem behaviors. However, Behavior Chains should also be used for effective decisions, as these also deserve inspection and reinforcement.

Graduation Transition Plan

It is important that teenage clients are well prepared and set up for success when they graduate from a DBT program. The Graduation Transition Plan is a worksheet to help teens prepare for graduation. This will help teens practice thinking ahead and to be prepared for stressors. Teens will also be asked to identify ways to build structure and be effective during the time they would typically be in group.

Commitment to DBT

By signing this form, I am making a commitment to DBT. I commit to:

1. Work on improving my safety, including Suicidal Ideation (SI) and Self-Injurious Behavior (SIB). This means that I will report on SI and SIB honestly and accurately. This also means that I will create skills plans and will be willing to learn and try skills to manage SI and SIB urges to keep myself safe.

2. Identify and problem solve my Therapy-Interfering Behavior (TIB). This means that I will be open to noticing and addressing my behaviors that get in the way of being at DBT, learning skills or making progress on my goals.

3. Set goals and take steps (even small ones) toward improving my life.

4. Follow group rules and expectations.

5. Actively participate in my DBT skills group and individual therapy. This means that I will work together with my therapists and group to learn skills and apply them to my life.

Signing this form also means that I will talk to my therapist(s) if I change my mind about DBT or I feel uncertain about my commitment to DBT.

_____

Client Name (printed)

_____   _____

Client Signature   Date

_____   _____

Therapist Signature   Date

_____   _____

Therapist Signature   Date

DBT Skills Group Rules and Expectations

Please read the following groups rules and expectations. Group members are responsible for knowing and following these rules and expectations.

Group members are expected to use their Wise Mind to act respectfully and Effectively in the group, even if a situation comes up that is not specifically mentioned in the following list:

- **Confidentiality:** Group members are expected to keep information about other members private. This means not sharing other group members' names outside of group or telling people outside of group who is in group. Confidentiality also means keeping personal information in group. Breaking confidentially may lead to discharge from this DBT program. Therapists are required to break your confidentiality if you or another minor is not safe. This means that your therapist has to report information about you or another minor being hurt or neglected by a parent or other adult.

- **Communication With Parents:** Therapists will try to keep what you share in group private from your parents or guardians. It is important that you know that your parents have a legal right to your information. Therapists will use their discretion in what is shared with your parents. In most cases, your therapist will try to include you in conversations with your parents. If there is a significant safety concern (where your therapist is concerned that you may act on suicidal thoughts or self-injury that would cause serious harm), your parents may be informed. Therapists will attempt to involve you in these conversations if possible.

- **Safety:** Members are not allowed to act on Suicidal Ideation (SI) or urges for Self-Injurious Behavior (SIB) while on premises: Doing so would be grounds for discharge from the program. Group members must not contact each other when in a crisis or depend on each other for safety needs. Group members must not share any details of SI or SIB or details about other topics that could be triggering. Therapists are required to report situations in which you are in danger or if you are being neglected.

- **Relationships With Group Peers:** Group members can use each other for support outside of group, but members are expected to be clear and respectful of each others' boundaries. Members are not allowed to have romantic or other private relationships with each other. What members talk about to each other outside of group must be able to be brought into group and talked about with everyone. Members are not allowed to use alcohol, drugs or participate in other unhealthy behaviors together. Participating in these behaviors together may lead to discharge. Members are not allowed to talk to each other about details of SI, SIB or TIB and are not allowed to engage in these behaviors together.

- **Attendance:** Group members are expected to attend every group. Members are expected to plan ahead and inform the therapist and group of absences as soon as possible.

- **Participation:** Group members are expected to actively participate. This means skillfully and effectively listening, giving feedback to others, contributing to teaching, doing a Diary Card and completing Behavior Chains and homework as assigned. This also means actively learning and using DBT skills in group and outside of group.

- **Feedback and Behavior:** Group members' feedback and behavior is expected to be respectful at all times. If a group member is disrespectful, a verbal warning will be given and he or she may be asked to leave or take a break from group. Disrespectful feedback and behavior includes:

    ○ Interrupting others

    ○ Yelling or using inappropriate verbal or nonverbal language

    ○ Using judgmental words or violating the boundaries of others

- **Cell Phones and Electronics:** Group members are expected to put their phones and other electronic devices on silent or turn them off during group. Group members may not use electronics, talk on the phone or text during group. Group members may be asked to turn in their devices if they cannot respect this rule.

- **Drugs and Alcohol:** Group members are not allowed to come to group under the influence of drugs or alcohol or use drugs or alcohol on premises and must not have drugs, alcohol or paraphernalia on premises. These behaviors are grounds for discharge. Group members may not glamorize the use of drugs or alcohol, and discussion about drugs and alcohol is expected to be effective during group and while on premises.

- **Treatment Team:** Group members are required to participate in ongoing individual therapy and are expected to comply with prescribed medications and recommendations from psychiatrists and medical professionals. Group facilitators will contact members of your team regularly to check in about your progress in therapy.

_____

Client Name (printed)

_____   _____

Client Signature   Date

My Crisis Survival Plan

It is time for me to turn to my Crisis Survival skills when:

1. _____
2. _____

This is how I can use the **Wise Mind ACCEPTS** skill to deal with my crisis:

1. _____
2. _____

This is how I can use the **Self-Soothe** skill to deal with my crisis:

1. _____
2. _____

This is how I can use the **IMPROVE the Moment** skill to deal with my crisis:

1. _____
2. _____

This is how I can use the **Creative Outlet** skill to deal with my crisis:

1. _____
2. _____

I can also use a **Half-Smile** to deal with my crisis.

These are people I can call for support:

1. Name: Phone Number:

2. Name: Phone Number:

3. Name: Phone Number:

I commit to follow my crisis survival plan. If I cannot keep myself safe, I commit to calling 911.

_____   _____

Client Signature   Date

_____   _____

Therapist Signature   Date

My Safety Contract

I commit to follow My Safety Contract to stay safe. I will use these DBT skills to help me deal with suicidal ideation and urges for self-harm:

1. _____

2. _____

3. _____

4. _____

5. _____

I can talk to these people if I need help following My Safety Contract:

1. Name: Phone Number:

2. Name: Phone Number:

3. Name: Phone Number:

I will try the skills on My Safety Contract, and if they do not help me stay safe with my Suicidal Ideation, I will call 911 and make sure I'm seen at the hospital. I will also call 911 and be seen at the hospital if I do not think I can avoid serious or life-threatening self-injury.

_____   _____

Client Signature   Date

_____   _____

Therapist Signature   Date

Adolescent DBT Diary Card

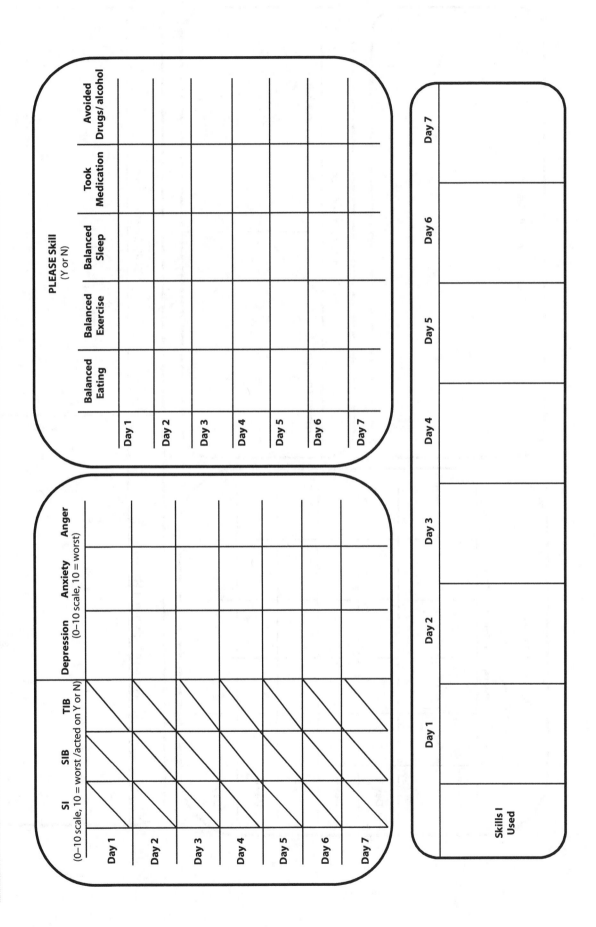

SI SIB TIB (0–10 scale, 10 = worst / acted on Y or N) **Depression Anxiety Anger** (0–10 scale, 10 = worst)

				Depression	Anxiety	Anger
Day 1						
Day 2						
Day 3						
Day 4						
Day 5						
Day 6						
Day 7						

PLEASE Skill (Y or N)

	Balanced Eating	Balanced Exercise	Balanced Sleep	Took Medication	Avoided Drugs/ alcohol
Day 1					
Day 2					
Day 3					
Day 4					
Day 5					
Day 6					
Day 7					

	Day 1	Day 2	Day 3	Day 4	Day 5	Day 6	Day 7
Skills I Used							

How I used Build Mastery

Build Positive Experiences

Positives I noticed:

Positives I created:

My Relationships
(0–10 scale, 10 = excellent)

	Self	Peers	Friends	Parents	Family
Day 1					
Day 2					
Day 3					
Day 4					
Day 5					
Day 6					
Day 7					

Skills for Stressors

Current or Upcoming Stressors

DBT Skills List

Mindfulness Skills

OBS	Observe	Pay attention; notice what is happening inside and outside yourself
DES	Describe	Put words on what you noticed
PART	Participate	Be active and engage in your experience
NJS	Non-Judgmental Stance	Focus on the facts; avoid labels or judgments
OM	One-Mindfully	Focus on one thing in the moment; be in the here and now
EFF	Effectively	Do what works; use skills

Distress Tolerance Skills

Crisis Survival Skills

DIST	Wise Mind ACCEPTS	Distract yourself; focus away from what is stressful
SS	Self-Soothe	Use your five senses to feel comforted and nurtured
ITM	IMPROVE the Moment	Replace difficult events with enjoyable events
HS	Half-Smile	Put a small smile on your face
CO	Creative Outlet	Put your emotional energy into creativity

Accepting Reality Skills

P&C	Pros and Cons	List the pros and cons
RA	Radical Acceptance	Accept what you cannot change; focus on what you can change
TTM	Turn the Mind	Change your thoughts so that you can accept
WI	Willingness	Do the best you can with what you have

Emotion Regulation Skills

PL	PLEASE	Take care of your physical health; self-care
BM	Build Mastery	Do things that help you to feel confident, capable and in control
JA	Just Act	Be active and get a task done
GMC	Give Myself Credit	Focus on your accomplishments
BPE	Build Positive Experiences	Do things that create enjoyable emotions; have fun!
O2E	Opposite to Emotion	Do the opposite of what your difficult emotion tells you to do
FYF	Feel Your Feelings	Let your emotions naturally come and go

Interpersonal Effectiveness Skills

A2R	Attend to Relationships	Care for your relationships
G	GIVE	Focus on what the other person needs; build healthy relationships
DM	DEAR MAN	Assert yourself; ask for what you want; say no
F	FAST	Focus on your self-respect in relationships

TIB Worksheet

Therapy-Interfering Behaviors (TIBs) are behaviors that:

- Get in the way of coming to therapy

- Get in the way of working with your therapist and group

- Get in the way of reaching your therapy goals

- Distract you from using DBT skills

- Are old ways of dealing with stress that make life worse

Examples of TIB includes:

- Skipping skills group or individual therapy

- Not participating in skills group or individual therapy

- Fighting in skills group

- Being distracted or distracting others in skills group

- Coming late or leaving therapy early

- Not taking medication as prescribed

- Not going to the doctor when sick

- Drinking alcohol or doing drugs

- Being willful

There are bound to be things that get in the way of therapy. Remember to have a Non-Judgmental Stance with your TIB and focus on brainstorming skills you can use to deal with your TIB.

Write down your TIBs here:

- _____

- _____

- _____

- _____

- _____

Keep track of your TIBs on your Diary Card. Notice when you have an urge to act on a TIB and remember that just because you have an urge for a TIB, you can make a choice to not act on it.

Emotion Words

HAPPY	SAD	WEAK	STRONG	CONFUSED	CALM	SCARED	ANGRY
Alive	Awful	Embarrassed	Able	Awkward	Chill	Afraid	Agitated
Amused	Bad	Exhausted	Active	Baffled	Collected	Anxious	Annoyed
Cheerful	Bummed	Fragile	Angry	Bewildered	Composed	Apprehensive	Burned
Content	Burnt out	Inadequate	Bold	Dazed	Content	Cautious	Disgusted
Delighted	Crushed	Incapable	Brave	Disorganized	Cool	Fearful	Fed up
Ecstatic	Depressed	Insecure	Capable	Disoriented	Easygoing	Frightened	Frustrated
Energized	Desperate	Powerless	Confident	Lost	Low key	Hesitant	Furious
Excited	Devastated	Resigned	Determined	Mixed up	Mellow	Horrified	Hateful
Fortunate	Disappointed	Run down	Eager		Peaceful	Insecure	Hostile
Fantastic	Disturbed	Self-conscious	Energized		Quiet	Intimidated	Inpatient
Friendly	Down	Useless	Healthy		Relaxed	Jumpy	Irate
Gleeful	Gloomy	Worn out	Powerful		Relieved	Nervous	Irritated
Good	Hopeless		Solid		Resting	Panicked	Livid
Great	Hurt		Spirited		Settled	Self-conscious	Mad
Hopeful	Lonely		Super		Still	Shaky	Miffed
Optimistic	Lost		Sure		Sure	Tense	Outraged
Overjoyed	Low		Tough		Tranquil	Terrified	Perturbed
Pleased	Miserable					Threatened	Riled up
Proud	Terrible					Timid	Resentful
Pumped	Unhappy					Uneasy	Ticked off
Satisfied	Unloved					Unsure	Worked up
Thankful						Worried	
Thrilled							
Warm							
Wonderful							

Behavior Chain

Each behavior is the result of a chain of events. A behavior chain is a way for you to look back at an effective or ineffective decision to help you figure out why and how you made your decision and where you had opportunities to apply DBT skills.

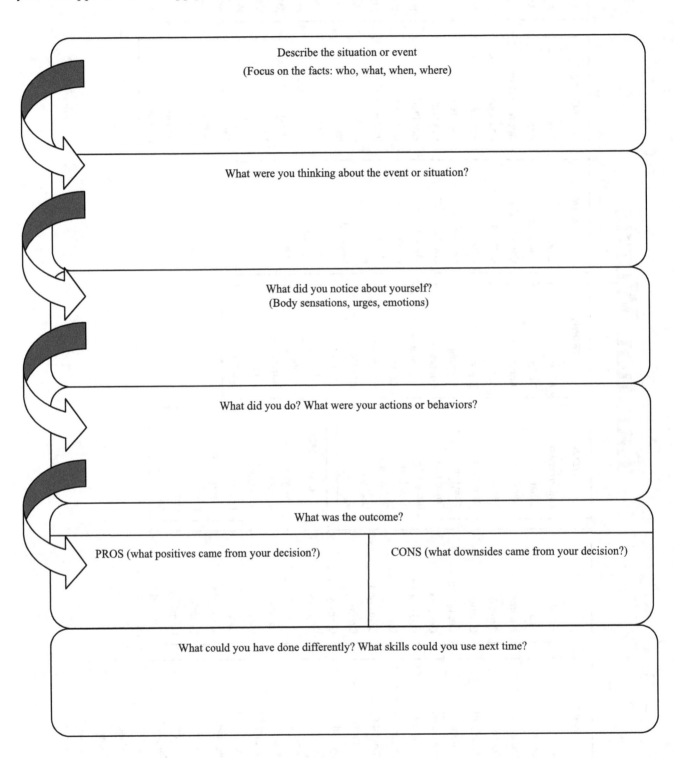

Describe the situation or event
(Focus on the facts: who, what, when, where)

What were you thinking about the event or situation?

What did you notice about yourself?
(Body sensations, urges, emotions)

What did you do? What were your actions or behaviors?

What was the outcome?

| PROS (what positives came from your decision?) | CONS (what downsides came from your decision?) |

What could you have done differently? What skills could you use next time?

Graduation Transition Plan

It is important to think ahead and make a plan to be successful without your DBT skills group. This worksheet will help you prepare for your graduation from DBT.

What problems did you come to DBT with?	How did DBT help you with those problems?

What areas do you still need to work on? Where do you need the most help?

What areas do you need the least amount of help with?

What do you think will be difficult after graduation?	What DBT skills can you use to help?

Who are your support people?

What can you do to build structure and replace your time spent in skills group?

Source Citations for DBT Modules, Skills, Worksheets & Activities

Part One: DBT for Teens

Dialectics (Linehan, 1993a & Linehan, 1993b)

Mindfulness Module (Linehan, 1993b)

States of Mind (Linehan, 1993b)

The "What" Skills (Linehan, 1993b)

Observe, Describe & Participate (Linehan, 1993b)

The "How" Skills (Linehan, 1993b)

Non-Judgmental Stance (Linehan, 1993b)

One-Mindfully (Linehan, 1993b)

Effectively (Linehan, 1993b)

Distress Tolerance Module (Linehan, 1993b)

Crisis Survival Skills (Linehan, 1993b/adapted by Eich, 2014)

Wise Mind ACCEPTS (Linehan, 1993b)

Self-Soothe (Linehan, 1993b)

IMPROVE the Moment (Linehan, 1993b)

Half-Smile (Linehan, 1993b)

Creative Outlet (Eich, 2014)

Accepting Reality Skills (Linehan, 1993b/adapted by Eich, 2014)

Pros and Cons (Linehan, 1993b)

Radical Acceptance (Linehan, 1993b)

Turn the Mind (Linehan, 1993b)

Willingness & Willfulness (Linehan, 1993b)

Emotion Regulation Module (Linehan, 1993b)

What Do You Believe About Emotions? (Linehan, 1993b/adapted by Eich, 2014)

Emotions: The Basics (Linehan, 1993b/adapted by Eich, 2014)

Why Do We Have Emotions? (Linehan, 1993b/ adapted by Eich, 2014)

Primary & Secondary Emotions (Linehan, 1993b/ adapted by Eich, 2014)

Emotions: The Big Picture (Linehan, 1993b/adapted by Eich, 2014)

Be an Emotions Detective (Eich, 2014)

PLEASE (Linehan, 1993b)

Build Mastery (Linehan, 1993b)

Just Act (Eich, 2014)

Give Myself Credit (Eich, 2014)

Build Positive Experiences (Linehan, 1993b)

100 Ways to Build Positive Experiences (Linehan, 1993b/adapted by Eich, 2014)

Opposite to Emotion (Linehan, 1993b)

Feel Your Feelings (Linehan, 1993b/adapted by Eich, 2014)

Interpersonal Effectiveness Module (Linehan, 1993b)

What Do You Believe About Relationships? (Linehan, 1993b/adapted by Eich, 2014)

Interpersonal Skills: The Basics (Linehan, 1993b/ adapted by Eich, 2014)

Balance Independence & Support (Miller, Rathus, Linehan, 2007/adapted by Eich 2014)

Balance Priorities & Demands (Linehan, 1993b/ adapted by Eich, 2014)

Ways to Practice Interpersonal Effectiveness Skills (Linehan, 1993b/adapted by Eich, 2014)

Attend To Relationships (Linehan, 1993b/adapted by Eich, 2014)

GIVE (Linehan, 1993b)

DEAR MAN (Linehan, 1993b)

FAST (Linehan, 1993b)

Boundaries (Pederson, 2012/adapted by Eich, 2014)

Part 2: DBT for Parents

Dialectical Dilemmas (Miller, Rathus, Linehan, 2007/adapted by Eich 2014)

What Is Typical, What Is Not? (Miller, Rathus, Linehan, 2007/adapted by Eich 2014)

Problem Behaviors (Miller, Rathus, Linehan, 2007/ adapted by Eich 2014)

Being Strict vs. Lenient (Miller, Rathus, Linehan, 2007/adapted by Eich 2014)

Independence vs. Support (Miller, Rathus, Linehan, 2007/adapted by Eich 2014)

Acceptance is Key (Linehan, 1993b/adapted for parenting by Eich, 2014)

Turn the Mind: Move Forward with Acceptance (Linehan, 1993b/ adapted for parenting by Eich, 2014)

Parenting from Wise Mind (Linehan, 1993b/ adapted for parenting by Eich, 2014)

Find Your Wise Mind in a Crisis (Linehan, 1993b/ adapted for parenting by Eich, 2014)

Feel Your Feelings (Linehan, 1993b/adapted by Eich, 2014)

Skills for Mindful Parenting (Linehan, 1993b/ adapted for parenting by Eich, 2014)

Observe, Describe & Participate (Linehan, 1993b)

One-Mindfully (Linehan, 1993b)

Non-Judgmentally (Linehan, 1993b)

Effectively (Linehan, 1993b)

GIVE: Put Relationship First (Linehan, 1993b)

DEAR MAN: Limit Setting (Linehan, 1993b)

Stick to Your Values (Linehan, 1993b)

PLEASE: Care for your Physical Health (Linehan, 1993b)

CARES: A Skill for Consistency (Eich, 2014)

Part 3: Therapist's Guide

Dialectical Dilemmas (Miller, Rathus, Linehan, 2007/adapted by Eich 2014)

Independence vs. Support (Miller, Rathus, Linehan, 2007/adapted by Eich 2014)

Being Strict vs. Lenient (Miller, Rathus, Linehan, 2007/adapted by Eich 2014)

Developmental Tasks vs. Problem Behaviors (Miller, Rathus, Linehan, 2007/adapted by Eich 2014)

Parental Involvement vs. Therapeutic Privacy (Eich, 2014)

Activity: Observe, Describe & Participate (similar to "Texture Exercise," Miller, Rathus, Linehan, 2007/expanded by Eich, 2014)

Activity: One-Mindfully (Eich, 2014)

Activity: Non-Judgmental Stance (similar to "What's in a Face?" Miller, Rathus, Linehan, 2007/expanded by Eich, 2014)

Activity: Wise Mind ACCEPTS

Board Game Day (Eich, 2014)

Create a Card (Eich, 2014)

TV Comparisons (Eich, 2014)

Distract with Humor (Eich, 2014)

Worry Box (Similar to "Worry Box, Callahan, 2008)

Alphabet Animals (Similar to "Last Letter, First Letter," Miller, Rathus, Linehan, 2007)

That's Sense-Sational! (Eich, 2014)

Activity: Self-Soothe (Similar to Self Soothe Kit, Christianson, Riddoch & Eggers-Huber, 2009)

Activity: IMPROVE the Moment

My Happy Place Collage (Eich, 2014)

Silver Linings List (Eich, 2014)

My Prayer Options (Eich, 2014)

Spa DBT (Similar to Self Soothe activity described in Miller, Rathus, Linehan, 2007)

One Piece at a Time (Eich, 2014)

Let's Take a Trip (Eich, 2014)

You Can Do It! I Can Do It! (Eich, 2014)

Jenga® (Jenga is a registered trademark of Pokonobe Associates)

Activity: Creative Outlet (Eich, 2014)

Activity: Turn the Mind (Eich, 2014)

Activity: Emotions: The Big Picture (Eich, 2014)

Activity: Event Cards (Eich, 2014)

Activity: Observe & Describe Emotions (Similar to Emotion Regulation activity described in Miller, Rathus, Linehan, 2007)

Activity: PLEASE (Eich, 2014)

Activity: Build Mastery (Eich, 2014)

Activity: Build Mastery: Group Goals (Eich, 2014)

Activity: Feel Your Feelings (Similar to Emotion Regulation activity described in Miller, Rathus, Linehan, 2007)

Activity: Types of Communication (Eich, 2014)

Activity: Scenario & Unskillful Communication Cards (Eich, 2014)

Activity: GIVE (Eich, 2014)

Activity: Our GIVE Chart (Eich, 2014)

Activity: Validation Scenarios List (Eich, 2014)

Activity: DEAR MAN Scenarios List (Eich, 2014)

Activity: FAST Scenarios List (Eich, 2014)

Activity: Values (Eich, 2014)

Sample Document: Commitment to DBT (Linehan, 1993b, Miller, Rathus, Linehan, 2007/ adapted by Eich, 2014)

Sample Document: DBT Skills Group Rules & Expectations (Pederson, 2012/adapted by Eich, 2014)

Sample Document: My Crisis Survival Plan (Pederson, 2012/adapted by Eich, 2014)

Sample Document: My Safety Contract (Pederson, 2012/adapted by Eich, 2014)

Sample Document: Adolescent DBT Diary Card (Linehan, 1993b, Miller, Rathus, Linehan, 2007/adapted by Eich, 2014)

Sample Document: DBT Skills List (Pederson, 2012/adapted by Eich, 2014)

Sample Document: TIB Worksheet (Eich, 2014)

Sample Document: Behavior Chain (Miller, Rathus, Linehan, 2007/adapted by Eich, 2014)

Sample Document: Graduation Transition Plan (Pederson, 2012/adapted by Eich, 2014)

For your convenience, you may download a PDF version of the Worksheets in this book from our website: **go.pesi.com/DBT**

Bibliography

Callahan, C. (2008). *Dialectical behavior therapy: children & adolescents.* Premier Publishing & Media: Eau Claire, WI.

Callahan, C. (2009). *Treatment of depression in children & adolescents.* Premier Publishing & Media: Eau Claire, WI.

Christensen, K., Riddoch, G. N. & Eggers-Huber, J. (2009). *Dialectical behavior therapy skills, 101 mindfulness exercises and other fun activities for children and adolescents: A learning supplement.* AuthorHouse: Bloomington, IN.

Dimeff, L. A. & Koerner, K. (2007). *Dialectical behavior therapy in clinical practice: Applications across disorders and settings.* Guilford Press: New York.

Duncan, B., Miller, S., Wampold, B. & Hubble, M. (2010). *The heart and soul of change: Delivering what works in therapy, 2nd ed.* American Psychological Association: Washington D. C.

Emmons, H. & Kranz, R. (2006). *The chemistry of joy.* Fireside: New York.

Epstein, S. P. (2012). *Over 60 techniques, activities & worksheets for challenging children and adolescents.* Premier Publishing & Media: Eau Claire, WI.

Gordon-Sheets, M. (2009). *Out-of-control: A dialectical behavior therapy (DBT)–cognitive behavioral therapy (CBT) workbook for getting control of our emotions and emotion-driven behavior.* Recovery Works Publications: Big Spring, TX.

Greco, L. A. & Hayes, S. C. (2008). *Acceptance and mindfulness treatments for children & adolescents: A practitioner's guide.* New Harbinger Publications: Oakland.

Linehan, M. M. (1993a). *Cognitive-behavioral treatment of borderline personality disorder.* Guilford Press: New York.

Linehan, M. M. (1993b). *Skills training manual for treating borderline personality disorder.* Guilford Press: New York.

Marra, T. (2005). *Dialectical behavior therapy in private practice: A practical and comprehensive guide.* New Harbinger Press: Oakland.

McKay, M., Wood, J. C. & Brantley, J. (2007). *The dialectical behavior therapy skills workbook: Practical DBT exercises for learning mindfulness, interpersonal effectiveness, emotion regulation & distress tolerance.* New Harbinger Press: Oakland.

McNeely, C.A. and Blanchard, J. (2010). *The Teen Years Explained: A Guide to Healthy Adolescent Development.* Baltimore, MD: Johns Hopkins University.

Miller, A. L., Rathus, J. H. & Linehan, M. M. (2007). *Dialectical behavior therapy with suicidal adolescents.* Guilford Press: New York.

Moonshine, C. (2008). *Acquiring competency & achieving proficiency with dialectical behavior therapy: Volume I–the clinician's guide book.* PESI: Eau Claire, WI.

Moonshine, C. (2008). *Acquiring competency & achieving proficiency with dialectical behavior therapy: Volume II–the worksheets.* PESI: Eau Claire, WI.

Pederson, L. (2012). *The expanded dialectical behavior therapy skills training manual.* Premier Publishing & Media: Eau Claire, WI.

Spradlin, S. E. (2003). *Don't let your emotions run your life: How dialectical behavior therapy can put you in control.* New Harbinger Press: Oakland.

Van Dijk, S. (2011). *Don't let your emotions run your life for teens: Dialectical behavior therapy skills for helping you manage mood swings, control angry outbursts get along with others.* New Harbinger Press: Oakland.